A play

Helen Blakeman

Samuel French — London
New York - Toronto - Hollywood

CARAVAN

First presented at the Bush Theatre, London on 12th November 1997 with the following cast:

Kim	Samantha Lavelle
Kelly	Emma Cunniffe
Josie	Elizabeth Estensen
Mick	Nick Bagnall
Bruce	Pip Donaghy

Directed by Gemma Bodinetz
Designed by Bruce Macadie
Lighting by Rick Fisher

CHARACTERS

Kim
Kelly
Josie
Mick
Bruce

The women of the play are from the south Liverpool suburbs, the men are from north Liverpool

The action takes place on a caravan park in Towyn, North Wales

Time — 1994-1996

SYNOPSIS OF SCENES

ACT I

SCENE 1   The caravan. A rainy afternoon in October 1994

SCENE 2   The following morning

SCENE 3   An evening in early March 1995

SCENE 4   A bright evening in September 1995

ACT II

SCENE 1   A dull afternoon, March 1996

SCENE 2   The following morning

SCENE 3   A bright summer Tuesday, 1996

SCENE 4   The following evening

SCENE 5   An early evening in late September 1996

To my family
and all those who've helped me along the way

ACT I

A caravan park in Towyn, North Wales

The set should consist of the cross-section of a caravan and the small piece of land in front of it. The action inside the caravan takes place in the main living area. The interior consists of two settees, a convertible bed, a cupboard, table and a small kitchen area. Three doors lead off the room, to the bathroom, Josie's room and Kelly's room. The window of Kelly's room faces out to the audience

Scene 1

Caravan of Love

Music: "Caravan of Love" by the Housemartins

The caravan, aged ten. A young static made of corrugated metal, painted cream and subdued orange with a pale blue stripe. Her concrete stilts and rusty chains tie her down. She thinks her "For Sale" sign could change her life — or at least her interior

A rainy afternoon in October 1994. A "For Sale" sign stands in the garden area outside the caravan. Two gas canisters stand near the steps up to the front door. The caravan is empty, although the table is scattered with newspapers, crockery and food — mostly packets of biscuits and bags of fruit. The convertible couch-bed displays a child's duvet cover. A cuddly Garfield toy sits on the pillow

Kim enters quickly, crosses to the door and enters the caravan. She is aged fifteen, fairly tall and rather busty. Sparky in temperament yet sensitive in nature. She dreams of better things. Kim is dressed for summer — a swimsuit, skirt and pumps — with a jacket over her head. Once inside the caravan, she throws the jacket on to the side settee. She straightens the bedclothes and hides the Garfield toy under the sheets. She embarks on tidying the table

Mick enters. He is aged twenty. Swarthy and casual. He has small hands and short legs. Can overpower but is very insecure. He takes whatever is given.

He is casually dressed and slightly wet. He carries two ice-creams — one is half-eaten

Mick (*calling*) Kim!

Kim goes to the door

Kim Are ya dead wet?

Mick enters the caravan

Mick Nah, I run fast.
Kim D'ya want some money for that?
Mick No.
Kim Ya sure?
Mick Don't be soft.
Kim Ta.

Mick goes to the back settee and looks about. Kim sits on the edge of the bed, as if trying to hide the duvet

Mick Is this ya mam an' dad's?
Kim We got it out the *Echo*. I 'aven't got a dad.
Mick It's not bad.
Kim Me mum loves it. She thinks it's dead nice. Every time she comes in she goes, "Ooh, me little palace". She wants to buy it an' everythin'.
Mick That'd be orright.
Kim Ya jokin' aren't ya? I'd go off me 'ead comin' 'ere all the time with me mum an' me sister. (*She licks the ice-cream*) This is lovely.
Mick I like mint choc chip.
Kim Cold though. (*Pause*) I'd rather stay at 'ome an' go out than come 'ere. I'd rather go to town, wouldn't you?
Mick I dunno. Depends.
Kim Depends on the company.
Mick Depends what's 'appenin'.
Kim What am I like? Depends. She 'asn't even bought it yet.
Mick So ya think she'll buy it then.
Kim Dunno, depends. Depends on the money. (*Pause*) Fancy 'avin' ice-cream in the rain.
Mick Cold an' wet.
Kim Yeh, cold an' wet an' nothin' goin' on just loadsa sheep an' one-arm bandits.
Mick That club's good. Ya should go. Three pound an' a bottle a Pils. An' birds get in for nothin'. Ya still get ya Pils like but ya can 'ave that in a

ladies' glass. Or ya can drink it out the bottle if ya drink it out the bottle.
Ya should go.
Kim I'll 'ave to see what are Kelly's doin'. We always go out together on
a Sat'dee.
Mick Whatever yeh.

Pause

Kim Where are ya sittin'? 'Ere or there?
Mick I'm sittin' 'ere.
Kim I'll sit 'ere as well then.

Kim sits alongside Mick on the back settee

I'm freezin'.
Mick Ya wanna put some clothes on.
Kim I'm orright.
Mick It's blowin' a gale.
Kim It was nice this mornin'.
Mick Not that I'm complainin'. Ya suit that … (*He gestures*)
Kim Cozzie.
Mick Yeh.
Kim Look at me. Goosies everywhere.
Mick You've got all ice-cream on ya chin.
Kim There?
Mick No. By ya mouth. Come 'ere.

Mick moves closer and wipes her chin

Kim Gone?
Mick No, there's more.

Kim moves away, embarrassed, and wipes her chin. She looks at her hand

Kim Where?
Mick It's on ya mouth.

*Mick puts his fingers on her mouth. Pause. He kisses Kim as she holds the
remains of her ice-cream at a distance*

Kim Should I shut the curtains?
Mick Nah, leave them.
Kim Ya can see in. Ya can see in to everyone's.

Mick Never noticed.

Kim stands and draws the curtains of the back and side windows

Kim Goin' dark now anyway.

Pause. They stand face to face

   D'ya wanna finish it?
Mick Yeh.

Mick takes the ice-cream from her. They kiss. He puts ice-cream on her lips then kisses it off

   That nice?
Kim Yeh.
Mick D' ya feel horny?
Kim Mm.
Mick I'm glad I went up the beach today.

He kisses her, still holding the ice-cream

   An' just when ya thought it was safe ——

He swiftly dabs ice-cream on to Kim's chest. She tries to back away

Kim Nah — you — Mick, oh my God — it feels dead cold get a cloth ——
Mick Leave it. Let me see it. Lie down.

Kim lies rigidly on the bed

   It looks better on ya chest than on ya chin.
Kim It's runnin' ——
Mick It's not.

He kneels astride Kim and leans down over her. He balances himself with one hand and holds the ice-cream with the other

   Mind ya arm.
Kim Mind that cornet.
Mick I am. I'm savin' it for somethin' special.
Kim Like what?
Mick Like you.

Mick kisses her neck and upper chest

Kim 'As it gone? (*Pause*) That tickles, slow.
Mick 'Old that.

Kim takes the ice-cream from him and holds it straight up above her. Mick resumes removing the ice-cream from her chest

Kim Ya like doin' that, don't ya?
Mick Mm.
Kim Can ya move up a bit? All ya weight's on me leg.

Mick moves slightly

　You sure ya comfy?
Mick Yeh. It's gorgeous.
Kim 'Ave ya finished?
Mick D' ya want some more?
Kim If ya want but 'urry up.

Mick kneels up and takes the ice-cream from Kim

Mick What time's ya mum in?
Kim Not for ages. They'll stop off at Rhyl for the bingo.
Mick We're all right then, aren't we?
Kim Watch it doesn't run out. I don't want no gunk on me bed. (*Pause*) Are ya gonna do any more?
Mick I'm tryin' to fuckin' eat.
Kim Keep ya kecks on. You 'aven't got ice-cream meltin' all over ya tit.

Mick puts the remains of the ice-cream in the bin and then resumes his position on top of Kim

Mick Ya feel good, don't ya?
Kim Yeh.
Mick Sexy cow.
Kim Ta.
Mick Turned on?
Kim Think so.
Mick Yeh?

They kiss passionately as Kim fumbles with Mick's flies

Kim Mick?

Mick What?
Kim I can't undo ya buttons.

Mick kneels and undoes his flies

Mick You're a horny bitch, d' ya know that?
Kim Mick?

They kiss

  Ow. Me back.
Mick Move over.

Mick reaches into the bed and pulls out the Garfield toy. He drops it on to the floor and kisses her

Kim Mick.
Mick I like this skirt. The way it goes right up.

Kim tugs her skirt down as Mick kisses her. She tries to move him off

Kim Mick, I've never ——
Mick It doesn't matter. You'll be orright.

He kneels again and loosens his jeans. He lies back down and fumbles with Kim's clothing

  Are these knickers?
Kim No, it's me cozzie.
Mick Move ya leg a bit. That's it. Can ya feel that?
Kim No. Leave it. Don't do that. No leave it now ——
Mick Move ya leg or we won't get nowhere ——

Mick's actions become more forceful

Kim God, no leave it now. That hurts. I don't want ——
Mick Move ya hand.
Kim Ow ——
Mick Let me pull it to the side ——
Kim Ah, no — don't do that — that hurts —
Mick That's it. That's better —
Kim Ow ——
Mick Just relax — relax a bit — open ya — ohh, that's it, that's better ——
Kim No, Mick, no — get off me now — get off get off me ——

Mick puts his hand over Kim's mouth to silence her. She struggles and groans then stiffens and becomes still

Mick Ohh, you're so fuckin' gorgeous — quiet now — orrhh, you'll make me come — Oh Kim — ah that's it — that's it — that's it — that's ohh — — (*He pulls away from her quickly*) Shit. I think some's gone on ya skirt.

He turns away from her and sits on the edge of the bed. Kim holds down her skirt

   D' ya think it was gonna be like that ya first time?
Kim Dunno.
Mick Ya were gorgeous.
Kim Thanks.
Mick Good the first time, innit?

Pause

Kim Was it all right?
Mick Yeh. I pulled out.
Kim Ta.
Mick Ya didn't 'alf get me goin' when ya groaned.
Kim It'll be orright, won't it?
Mick As long as I don't 'ave to bring flowers the 'ospital when it's born. I'd feel a cunt.

Kim stands and looks through the window, out front

Kim Not goin' the fair now. It's pissin' down.
Mick 'Ave to make it another time.
Kim It might go off in a bit.
Mick I'll 'ave to get off.

Kim edges her way towards the kitchen

Kim Stay. I'll do ya tea. We could 'ave noodles an' curry sauce with veg in.
Mick Me mam does me tea.
Kim With peas an' carrots. Like vegetable curry. We could get more ice-cream for afters.
Mick Ya mam'll be back. I'll 'ave to go.
Kim It'd be orright.
Mick I'm in a rush for goin' out. I might see ya later.
Kim Where are ya?

Mick Up the top.
Kim In millionaires' row? I've seen them. They've all got dralon couches.
I'll come an' knock. Where ya goin' after?

Josie enters on to the terrace in front of the caravan. She is aged forty-five.
Thin-faced and sharp-featured, she appears slimmer than she is. Ambition
only centres around material items. She thinks she has found better things.
She is loaded up with bags of bingo prizes and cuddly toys

Josie (*calling*) Kimberley, get 'old a these for us, babe.
Kim Shite.
Mick I'd better go. (*He goes to exit*)
Kim No — she'll go mad. You'll 'ave to get out the back winda.
Josie Give us a hand, love.

Kim guides Mick into Josie's room

Kim Go on. (*Calling*) I'm comin' now, Mum.
Mick If anyone sees me ——
Josie (*calling*) Kimmy?
Kim I've 'ad a lovely day. I'll see ya after or whatever.
Mick Ta-ra.

Mick exits from the back window of the caravan

Kim (*calling*) I'm comin'!
Josie Are you in, love? Open the door it's only ya mam.

Kim goes to the door and steps out

Kim I thought you'd 'ave ya keys. 'As it stopped rainin'?
Josie Just. We've 'ad a crackin' day, weather aside. Ya shoulda come. Ya
would've enjoyed ya little self. Grab 'old a them.

Josie enters the caravan

Kim So it was good then?

Kim re-enters the caravan, drops the bags and tidies her bed

Josie Got all me bags?
Kim Think so.
Josie I'm glad to be back. Me bleedin' feet are achin' off me. Are Kelly's

gone the "Amouré" for a pizza. Fuckin' pizza mad she is. You'd think she'd 'ave enough a them in work.

Kim Did ya stop off at Rhyl?

Josie Stop off? I cleaned the fuckin' town out. Lovely bus driver we 'ad. Like Omar Sharif but not as greasy. An' the bingo was fuckin' marvellous. I'll just get me slippers.

She exits to her bedroom

(*Off*) 'E took a shine to are Kelly. Kept callin' 'er "sweet 'eart". The couple sat behind us own one a these. Two rows down. They're 'ere every weekend peak season.

Josie re-enters the living-room wearing her slippers and sifts through her prizes. Kim sits on the edge of the bed, quite still

Imagine that, eh, Kim? Rhyl just down the road. The bingo, the bars. You could be clubbin' it down there next year. Make-up on, all dressed up. Are Kelly could take ya once she's passed 'er test. You'd pass for eighteen. You'd love it.

Kim Can I go out tonight?

Josie We were singin' on the way back. Omar didn't seem to care. They even 'ad a twistin' competition up the back. Didn't know till it was too late. I don't know who won but they wouldn't be as good as me, eh, babes? What you been up to then?

Kim Went up the beach, it was nice. Went the fair, it rained. Came back.

Josie Did ya meet ya nice friends from Frodsham?

Kim Yeh.

Josie Anyone new?

Kim No. I think someone else is in next door. They've got bikes an' everythin'.

Josie Just wait till I buy this place. I'll give them festoon blinds never mind bloody bikes. Bleedin' show-offs. Are Kelly can 'ave the make-up set. D'ya wanna teddy off the grabbers? Ee are, put that on ya bed. That'll cheer ya up.

Kim takes the cuddly toy and puts it on the pillow

Ya dad woulda loved today. What's that on ya skirt?

Kim What?

Josie The life an' soul of it, wasn't 'e, Kim?

Kim Where?

Josie That's one thing I'll say for 'im. All white stuff down the back.

Kim Dunno. Ice-cream.

Kim sits on the bed. Josie lights a cigarette

Josie I 'ope it comes out. When I get ya dad's 'oliday insurance, I'll bloody buy this place. An' them clouds'll part an' the sun'll come out an' ya dad'll be 'appy up there. 'E'll go, "Josie's got a caravan an' that's what she's always dreamed of". An' for once 'e'll be 'appy with me. We'll all be 'appy.

SCENE 2

Saturday Night

Music: "Saturday Night" by Whigfield

The caravan, the following morning

Kim is preparing breakfast for two at the still cluttered table. She places a banana, an apple and an orange on each plate. She is dressed as in Scene 1

Kim Ee are! (*She peels a banana and begins to eat it*) It's lovely this. Dead posh muesli with extra nuts an' loadsa bits in. (*Silence. This is a daily routine for her*) Ya milk's gettin' soaked up. If it goes all mushy it'll look like spew. So don't say I never warned ya. (*Silence. She clears most of the clutter from the table*) It's says on the packet, "Good for ya spots, good for ya shits, (*calling*) good for ya shags an' stops ya gettin' cancer." Not bad, eh? Bet ya didn't know muesli could change ya life? (*Pause*) Or would ya rather 'ave a sausage? I'd rather 'ave a sausage. (*Pause*) Come on. Are ya gettin' up or what? It's dead nice out.

Pause. The curtains of the front bedroom window open. Kelly, already dressed, looks out of the window

Right, Kelly. That's it. It's goin' in the cat. Why should I waste me mornin' waitin' for you when there's very important fish to fry?

Kelly enters from the bedroom carrying a make-up bag and hairbrush. She is aged nineteen. Dark-haired, sturdy and short. Appears gentle and naïve but is not as soft as she makes out. She looks for better things. She is dressed for attention but looks rather dishevelled

Kelly We 'aven't got a cat.

Kim It's just a phase, a figure a speech.

Kim passes Kelly a plate of fruit

Ee are. I was lyin' about the muesli.

Kelly I couldn't look at food. (*She sits down on the back settee*)

Kim That's nice. After I've gone to all that trouble arrangin' ya breakfast fruit in alphabetical order.

Kelly Is that why the orange is in the middle?

Kim Ya lookin' at it the wrong way round, clever arse. (*She puts the untouched fruit on the table*)

Kelly Oh, shut ya face.

Kim Yeh, when you shut ya neck.

Kelly Well shut ya legs.

Kim Shut ya aarse.

Kelly Ah, just shut up, Kim, me 'ead feels like it's on the waltzers.

Kim Put some make-up on. You'll feel human then. You'll still look like a dog but at least you'll feel human.

Kelly (*quietly*) Shut ya hole.

Kim I'm goin' the beach in a minute, ya comin'?

Kelly Don't think so.

Kim Well wait till ya spew then see 'ow ya feel. Or do ya hair. (*Pause*) I'll do ya hair. I'll do it nice. An' ya make-up. Ya can use them eye shadows off me mum. (*She picks up the make-up set*) "Earthy Shades" Earthy colours are in. (*She reads*) "Winter dawn, frosty peach, golden towny".

Kelly Tawny.

Kim Whatever. (*Pause*) Come 'ead, don't be an aald aarse. Come the beach.

Kelly It'll be bloody freezin'.

Kim So? Ya on 'oliday.

Kelly Are you goin' like that?

Kim Yeh. Why?

Kelly Ya skirt's all dirty.

Kim Shit. I forgot about that. (*She takes a small pile of clothes and a beach bag from a cupboard*)

Kelly begins to do her hair in a hand mirror. Through the following dialogue, Kim tries on various skirts and shorts over her costume

Kelly Did you know that ya only supposed to take five items a clothes on 'oliday with ya?

Kim Like what?

Kelly A cozzie, a sarong ——

Kim A what?

Kelly A big fancy sheet. A pair a shorts, a long skirt an' — (*she thinks*) somethin' else.

Kim Five bitsa clothes? Go 'way, you'd stink. (*Pause*) There was a dirty big turd on the beach yesterday.

Kelly Eugh. The dirty Welsh bastard.

Kim It wasn't Welsh shit, it was in the sea. (*Pause*) Everyone was runnin' away from it.

Kelly An' ya want me to come with ya?

Kim Just today. I don't wanna go on me own.

Kelly You've changed ya tune.

Kim Girls look better in twos. (*Pause*) An' one can mind the bags while the other one goes in for a paddle.

Kelly Ya must be jokin'. Paddlin' in squalid conditions? (*She sits*) Move over. (*She starts to make herself up*)

Kim (*picking up a skirt*) D' ya think this one or the shorts?

Kelly That one.

Kim Ya 'ave a laugh. (*Pause*) An' ya get a tan off the sea.

Kelly More like fuckin' beri-beri.

Kim No, ya do. If the wind's blowin'. Come with me, come on.

Kelly I can't. I'm goin' the fair ——

Kim We can go there after ——

Kelly To Rhyl?

Kim Who ya goin' there with?

Kelly Someone.

Kim Is it that Omar?

Kelly 'Ave I got taste?

Kim It's 'ard to say.

Pause

Kelly Someone from last night.

Kim From that stupid cabaret bar? Eeeh, only queers go in cabaret bars.

Kelly No. From Fortnum's on the coast road.

Kim Is that that club?

Kelly Yeh. Free to get in an' a bottle a Pils.

Kim I'll kill me mum. I can't go nowhere.

Kelly Ya wouldn't a got in, babe. Tell ya what, I'll take ya to town once ya sixteen.

Pause

Kim What was it like? Is it really, really brilliant?

Kelly It's orright. Not exactly the hottest spot north of Havana.

Kim But what like?

Kelly It was good. We 'ad a scream.

Kim I 'ate this. I 'ate this stupid 'oliday. Did ya cop for anyone?

Kelly Yeh. Sandra an' Lisa were up dancin', I was leanin' over watchin', an' this gorgeous lad comes up to me an' goes, "I don't 'alf know your face". An' that was it.

Kim What was?

Kelly I just started neckin' 'im.

Kim Ee, ya slapper.

Kelly Wait till you get a bit older.

Kim I'm old enough.

Kelly 'E even walked me 'ome. 'E's just gorgeous. Me 'eart was poundin' all the way.

Kim All the way?

Kelly All the way 'ome.

Kim I 'ate livin' with you an' me mum. Ya either dead narky or yers are makin' a show a yerself.

Kelly What's up your aarse, moaner?

Kim I get dragged up the bingo an' the family bar an' all the time you're shaggin' ——

Kelly Snoggin'.

Kim Is that all ya did? An' me mum (*she whispers*) mum was up doin' *Saturday Night* an' flirtin' with some stupid aald pig. An' when I went to bed she sneaked 'im in through the winda. I could 'ear them smoochin' an' laughin' an' doin' things.

Kelly That was me, soft shite.

Kim Ya brought 'im back 'ere?

Kelly We never done nothin' so don't be gettin' ideas.

Kim I thought it was me mum. I was prayin' to me dad an' Our Lady to make 'im go an' everythin'.

Kelly Well now ya know.

Kim Ya mean, ya brought 'im back 'ere an' never done nothin'?

Kelly No.

Kim Would ya a done if there was no-one in?

Kelly I've only just met 'im.

Kim I was only askin'.

Kelly Do I look all right? 'E'll be 'ere in a minute.

Kim What's 'is name?

Kelly Wait till ya meet 'im, Kim. 'E's like me dad, all gentle like — (*she thinks*) a gentleman.

Kim 'As 'e got a moustache?

Kelly No.

Kim Then why's 'e like me dad?

Kelly It was just the way 'e ett 'is chips.
Kim Did 'e get ya chips?
Kelly Yeh.
Kim It's nice isn't it, when they buy ya somethin' special.
Kelly 'Ow would you know?
Kim I just think it must be nice. (*Pause*) When's 'e comin' round?
Kelly Now, soon. In a minute!
Kim Does 'e wear trainees or shoes?
Kelly Twenny fuckin' questions! I don't know!
Kim Oh, I'm goin' the beach.
Kelly So ya said.

Josie enters from her bedroom. She wears silky pyjamas, a dressing-gown and slippers. She looks better than she feels. She stops and lights a cigarette

Kim Oh shut ya face.
Kelly Shut ya fadge.
Kim Yeh shut ya minge.
Kelly Shut ya tits.
Kim Shut ya mary.
Kelly Shut ya pits.
Josie Now don't go bringin' politics into it.
Kelly What?

Pause. Josie thinks

Josie I'm sure that HRT gets ya pissed.
Kim Don't give none to are Kelly then.

Josie sits at the table and surveys the clutter

Josie Should a brought more food with us.
Kelly Get some at the market.
Kim It's all second-'and cakes an' mouldy veg.
Kelly Does this top look stupid?
Kim Yeh.
Josie No.
Kelly Thanks a lot. I'm already late an' you're sayin' me top's mingin'.

Kelly exits to her bedroom

Josie Where's she goin'?
Kim The fair with some ug.

Josie So she copped?
Kim That's what she reckons. (*Pause*) She reckons she brought 'im back
   'ere.
Josie I thought I 'eard someone raspin' with passion outside my winda.
Kim I thought it was you an' that fella.
Josie Be'ave yerself. Ya dad's still warm.
Kim 'E kept slidin' 'is 'and down ya bum.
Josie We was 'avin' a laugh. Bruce is a nice fella.
Kim You went with someone called Bruce?
Josie Went with?
Kim Ya kissed 'im. I seen ya. I seen ya kissin' 'im.
Josie Just to say good-night.
Kim Ya were snoggin'. Propply snoggin'. I could see ya reflection in the
   arcade winda. Ya were laughin'. Ya were laughin' an' ya were kissin'. Ya
   were kissin' 'im an' ya 'ad ya hand on 'is arse. Ya were laughin'. Ya was,
   ya were laughin'. Ya stopped an' ya were laughin'. Ya make me sick. Ya
   just make me feel ill.

Pause

Josie So I should stay on me own the rest a me life ——
Kim There's no-one like me dad.
Josie An' not 'ave friends?
Kim Some friend!

There is a knock on the back of the caravan. Josie starts

Josie Who the shittinell's that?
Kim Kelly!

Kelly bursts from her bedroom wearing a different top

Kelly Shit. Is this top tight enough?
Josie Who is it?
Kelly (*calling*) It's open!

Mick crosses in front of the caravan and heads for the door

Kim It's are Kelly's fella.
Josie Didn't know I was runnin' an open bordello.

Kelly stands near the door facing Mick, on the steps

Kelly 'Iya.
Mick Thought I'd got the wrong one then.
Kelly Come in. I'm nearly ready.

Mick enters

Josie Come in, son. Sit down.
Mick I'm orright.
Kelly I won't be a minute.
Josie Take no notice a me in all me glory. The state a this place an' all. The shame of it. You'll think we're a gang a gyppos.

Kelly exits to her bedroom

Mick Ya orright.
Josie Introductions, Kelly.

Kelly appears round the bedroom door

Kelly That's me mum an' that's are Kim.

Kelly exits

Josie Sit down, love. I don't know ya name.
Mick Mick.
Josie Sit down, Mick. I'm Josie, by the way. Move up, Kimmy, let Mick sit down.

Kim moves along swiftly. Mick sits

Mick 'Iya.

Kim looks away

Josie Nice day for the fair.
Mick Not bad. A bit dull now.
Josie Weather's not bad, considerin'.
Mick No.
Josie Rhyl, is it?
Mick Yeh.
Josie Ya goin' on the bus?
Mick I've got me dad's car.
Josie Very nice. You'll 'ave to teach are Kelly.
Mick Yeh.

Kelly enters from the bedroom wearing a bumbag and carrying a small jacket

Ya ready then?

Kelly All cleaned up an' ready to rumble. (*Checking the contents of her bumbag*) Got me lippy, got me keys, got me money.

Josie (*forcefully*) An' don't go on them chair-o-planes.

Kelly As if I would.

Josie Ta-ra, Mick. See ya again, son. (*To Kim*) Say Ta-ra to Mick.

Kim Ta-ra.

Mick Nice to meet ya.

Kelly and Mick exit from the caravan

Josie Fancy are Kelly gettin' a bit of orright. I'm glad she's courtin'.

Kim Courtin'? 'E'll be with someone else tomorrow.

Josie You're just in a tizz, you are.

Kim I'm not.

Josie Well do somethin' with yerself an' don't sit there like a sack a spuds.

Kim I'm not.

Josie D' ya wanna come the market?

Kim I'm goin' the beach. I told ya last night I was goin' the beach.

Josie Eh! I like their 'angin' baskets. We'll 'ave them. This'll be a little palace when I get ya dad's insurance. All lovely fuchsias an' petulias. (*Pause*) Nice nets an' all.

Kim Nice yeh.

Josie Ah well, no use gawpin', better start buyin'.

Kim Curtains?

Josie Cushions. Cushions are a start. An' I'll get some a them out-of-date noodles if they sell them. At least that'll cheer ya up.

Josie exits to her bedroom

Kim sits. She sings a couple of lines from "Saturday Night" by Whigfield. She goes to her bed, picks up the quilt and sniffs it. She folds the quilt and pillows and places them on top of the bed with the cuddly toys. She sits at the end of the bed and looks forward. Pause

(*Calling*) Mum, 'ow long will ya be?

Josie (*off*) You go if ya want.

Kim goes to the table and clears the rest of the clutter

Kim (*calling*) I'll tidy up first.
Josie (*off*) Ta, Kimmy babes.

*Kim goes to the back settee. She picks up her bag and takes out a beach towel.
She places the towel on top of the pile of clothes and tidies them away in the
cupboard. She returns to sit on the edge of the bed*

Kim (*calling*) Mum.
Josie (*off*) What?
Kim (*calling*) Can I come the market with you?
Josie (*off*) I thought ya were goin' the beach.
Kim (*calling*) There's no point, the sun's gone in.

SCENE 3

Babies

Music: "Babies" by Pulp

The caravan. An evening in early March 1995

The caravan is empty

*Mick enters. He is followed by Kelly. She is dressed in an Asda supermarket
uniform and wears a jacket. Mick wears a sporty outdoor coat. They each
carry a case — Kelly's being much bigger than Mick's. She also carries a
small bag. Mick reaches the door of the caravan, stops and waits. Kelly hauls
her case along throughout her dialogue. She stops occasionally to change
hands or rest, then continues*

Kelly (*in disbelief*) An' then I 'eard it over the tannoy — "Congratulations
to Kelly on are fresh pizza counter — who got married to her fiancé Mick
yesterdee. — Congratulations, good luck, best wishes, all that — from
everyone in the store." Mick, I — felt — ashamed. Anyway, I was on
checkouts today so no-one knew it was me. None a the customers looked
at me "Kelly Happy to Help" badge and went — "Oooh, are you the one?"
— "Ah, it rained yesterdee didn't it?" — "Was it in a church? Fancy 'avin'
to work the day after." (*She picks up the case and quickly hobbles the last
few yards*) Uurgh, bloody 'ell! (*She stops*)
Mick Why don't ya just say?
Kelly (*still holding the case*) Say what?
Mick Ya shoulda carried mine. Why didn't ya say?
Kelly It's dead wifey. I didn't like ——

Mick (*picking up the case*) Jesus Christ, Kel. What's in 'ere?

Kelly Just essentials really.

Mick Bleedin' 'ell.

Kelly (*gesturing to the small bag*) There wasn't even room for the 'oneymoon food.

Mick The what food?

Kelly The randy food. Ya know, food that gets ya goin'.

Mick Ya what?

Kelly Chocolate spread, avocado pears and Chinese oyster sauce.

Mick Give me that an' I would be goin'. 'Ave ya got the keys?

Kelly Oyster sauce is nice. I 'ad it at the Ming Sing on me eighteenth.

Pause

Mick Kelly, where's the keys?

Kelly Oh yeh. I was gettin' them out, then I told ya about work an' I forgot. (*She reaches into the bag and brings out the keys*)

Mick Go on then. Open up.

Kelly offers the keys to Mick

It's your mam's caravan.

Kelly Not yet it's not.

Mick Ya know what I mean.

Kelly Sorry.

Kelly opens the door of the caravan, puts on the light and enters

Mick (*calling*) Didn't they 'ave a collection for us in work?

Kelly Who did?

Mick (*calling*) In work.

Kelly They're not that bloody quick. They might do when I go back. It smells dead musty, Mick, an' it's bloody freezin'. (*She opens the bedroom doors*)

Mick I 'ope so 'cos the dole don't believe in weddin' presents.

Kelly goes to the front door and takes the large case from Mick. She puts the case in Josie's room

Kelly Or they might do once I've 'ad the baby.

Mick enters the caravan with the small case and places it outside Josie's room. He then relaxes on the back settee

Mick That's for the kid, though, not for us.

Kelly takes the small case into Josie's room

Kelly It is for us. It's for us as well.
Mick 'Ave a rest now, Kel. Come on.

Kelly enters the living-room and takes a newspaper from her bag

Kelly Not much chance with you around. I got ya the paper.
Mick I don't want the paper. I want you.
Kelly Well 'ave it anyway.
Mick Sit down. Come 'ead. We 'aven't got long.
Kelly I thought we could keep it 'cos it's got the date on.
Mick Sit down. They'll be 'ere soon.
Kelly I am. I forgot to get one yesterday. But it doesn't matter. We'll keep this one so we know what 'appened the day after. (*She sits beside Mick*)
Mick Yeh, are honeymoon anniversary.
Kelly News that gets ya goin'.
Mick Ya shoulda got the *Sport*.
Kelly That's just tits.
Mick I know.

They kiss. Mick begins to undo Kelly's overall

Kelly I love ya, Mick.
Mick I know. (*He takes off his shoes*) I've been waitin' all day for a good shag off you, Mrs Maguire.

Kelly kicks off her shoes and lies down

Kelly I know what ya mean.
Mick Me bollocks are burstin'. (*He undoes his belt and flies*)
Kelly Were ya dead angry last night?
Mick I was dead 'orny.
Kelly I just don't like doin' it in me mum's.
Mick It'll be orright when we get a place.

Mick kneels on the settee in between Kelly's legs

Kelly It'll be brilliant.

Mick lowers himself down on top of Kelly. Pause

Mick I know.

They kiss

Kelly D'ya think it'll be different cos we're married?
Mick It'll be fuckin' excellent.

Mick fumbles with Kelly's overall as she tugs at his jeans

Kelly Shall I shut the curtains?
Mick Just leave them.
Kelly Shall we get on the floor?
Mick If ya want.

They tumble awkwardly to the floor, still trying to kiss

   You on top?
Kelly Yeh.

Kelly establishes herself on top of Mick

Mick 'Urry up. I just wanna put it in.
Kelly Ah, watch me knee.
Mick Take ya tights off.
Kelly I will now. Move a minute — ow.

Kelly stands and undoes the rest of her overall. Mick lies back, watching her

Mick Mind the winda.
Kelly (*turning off the light*) Flash 'Arry'll be 'avin' a waz like there's no
   tomorrow watchin' us.
Mick Just take it off, Kel.
Kelly I'm gonna be bleedin' freezin'. An' don't you groan too much. 'E'll
   get off on that an' all, the dirty screff.
Mick I couldn't give a shit.
Kelly I know. I'll put me goin' away outfit on. Then you can take it off again.
Mick Ya shoulda done it before.

Kelly takes a tiny, stretchy dress from her bag

Kelly Never 'ad time before. Ya can't get off them tills on a Friday.
Mick Just 'urry up, they'll be 'ere by seven.

Kelly takes off her overall and drops it round her feet. Her tights are more hole than gusset. She attempts to put on her dress

Kelly We've got ages yet. I didn't want ya to wait. Ya were good enough gettin' ya dad's car. I just wanted to get 'ere an' it be just you an' me.

Mick watches, amused, as Kelly battles with the dress. It is still round her shoulders

Not that it will be for long. I'm gonna be bleedin' freezin' in this. I forgot to pack me weddin' bra an' all. (*She tries unsuccessfully to squeeze it over her chest*) I shoulda got a twelve.

There is a noise outside the caravan. Kelly stops. Mick listens

The door opens. It is Josie and Kim

Christ! Who is it?
Josie Surprise, lovebirds!

Mike jumps up and starts to make himself decent. He sits on the settee. Kelly tugs down her dress

Kelly Oh my God.
Josie We managed to get the early train.
Kelly Mam! Ya said after seven.
Josie That's all right, isn't it?

Josie enters carrying a suitcase and puts on the light. Kim follows, wearing a track-suit. She carries a holdall and holds a cake box

You carry on doin' what ya doin'. Just pretend we're not 'ere.

Mick is still straightening himself. Kim stands near the door, still

Can ya manage that, Kimberley, love?
Mick D'ya need a hand?
Josie No, love. Do you? (*She puts down her case*)

Kim puts the box on the table. She marches past Kelly into Josie's bedroom with her holdall

Kelly "Sorry we're early. Did we disturb ya?"
Josie 'Aven't ya put the gas on? Christ, you'd freeze ya bits off in 'ere.

Josie takes the case into the front bedroom and places it inside

Kelly 'Aven't 'ad a chance.

Josie What time did ya get 'ere?

Kelly Before. (*She puts the overall in her bag*) Won't be seein' that again for a week.

Mick Ya not the only one. (*He lights a cigarette*)

Josie Done much?

Mick No.

Kelly There's nothin' open.

Josie Bruce said that. 'E's glad 'e's doin' double shifts. 'E said 'e'd rather do that than come 'ere.

Kelly So it'll be swingin' then.

Josie Oh, we can make are own fun, can't we? That's what I said to Bruce. Might as well be all of us in me lovely little palace, it's still the same price. We got ya a lovely cake, Kel. An' there's some cans an' a bottle a bucks fizz in the 'oldall.

Kim enters from the bedroom

Kim Why do we always come at crap times?

Josie Stop moanin'. This is a happy day.

Kim I'm not moanin'. It's me 'ormones.

Josie Kelly's 'ormones are in the same state as yours an' she's not moanin'.

Kim Well she's not sleepin' in the livin'-room, is she?

Josie It is their honeymoon. They deserve a bit a privacy.

Kim So do I. I've got mornin' sickness.

Kelly An' I 'aven't?

Josie Get in with me then.

Kim I'd rather spew in public.

Kim exits to Josie's bedroom

Josie (*calling*) Come on, we'll 'ave some cake. It's lovely sponge.

Kelly (*quietly*) I'm tellin' ya, Mum, she's not gonna spoil this week.

Mick (*eating*) Leave it, Kel.

Kelly I won't. I'll tell 'er.

Josie (*quietly*) Now leave it, she's depressed enough as it is.

Kim enters carrying a four-pack of lager

Kim Anyone want a can?

Mick Go 'ead, Kim.

Kim sits down next to Mick. They both click open their cans

Kelly What 'ave you been told about drinkin'?
Kim It gets ya pissed an' gives ya a red nose. Can I 'ave a drag on that?
Mick Ya can 'ave one if ya want.
Kim Ta.

Kim takes a cigarette from Mick and lights up

Kelly If ya both gonna smoke ya can sit over there.

Josie lights a cigarette

> (*Standing*) 'As nobody got respect for the unborn child? I'll move if ya
> don't mind.

Kelly crosses to the table and sits. Josie passes Kim a slice of cake

Josie D' ya know what? I'd rather cover meself in them expensive plasters
an' pretend they were doin' me good than put up with this moanin' for
another five months. Pass us that ashtray.

Kelly does so reluctantly

Kim We 'ad a gorgeous gateau at that pub last night.
Josie O, youse missed a lovely choice a puddin's.
Mick I was burstin' after the roast.
Josie I bet ya was.
Kelly Too much stodge is bad for ya anyway.
Josie Is that why ya went 'ome early, Mick? Ya couldn't wait to get it out
ya system.
Kelly It's tradition for the couple to go 'ome early from receptions. It is, isn't
it, Mick?
Mick I wouldn't know ——
Kim It wasn't a reception, anyway. It was a meal in a smelly pub.
Mick I thought we went 'ome 'cos you felt sick.
Kelly Well it is. It's tradition. (*Pause*) It's a wonder you never felt sick, all
the lambrusco you kept downin'.
Kim I can take me ale.
Kelly An' all the shite ya stuff down ya neck.
Josie Now don't start.
Kelly I'm not startin'. Just that she should 'ave more sense.

Kim I 'ave got sense. Who'd wanna get married in a poky little room? When it's my turn, I'm gettin' married on a beach.

Kelly Where? Ainsdale with all the shite? I'm talkin' sense, sense. Sense of responsibility. Sense of well-being. Sense of ya own mind. Sense of … (*She struggles*)

Kim Sense a humour? 'Cos you 'aven't got one. (*She laughs*)

Mick raises a smile

Kelly Oh, shut ya big fat aarse, you.
Josie Stop it.
Kim Shut yours.
Kelly Just shut ya tits.
Josie Very nice.
Kim At least I've got some.
Kelly Shut ya big fat, saggy, droopy tits.
Kim Shut ya fishole.
Josie Now me an' Mick 'ave 'ad enough a this.
Kelly Shut yours. I can smell it from 'ere, trawler fanny.
Josie I 'ope youse don't 'ave girls.

Kim stands and crosses towards the bathroom

Kim I 'ope we do 'cos mine'll be better lookin' than 'ers.
Kelly Cheeky runt.

Kim opens the door of the bathroom and enters half-way

Kim (*with venom*) Mrs Maguire!

Kim slams the door and locks it

Josie (*calling*) If ya told us who the father was, we might 'ave an idea of what it will look like.
Kim (*off*) I've told ya.
Josie (*calling*) You've told me nothin'.
Kim (*off*) 'E's fifteen.

Kelly crosses to sit by Mick

Kelly She does my 'ead in.
Josie (*calling*) Yeh an' I wanna know 'is name.
Kim (*off*) I've told ya. 'E's fifteen an' ya can't touch 'im.

Josie goes to the bathroom door

Are you listenin'? I'm tryin' to 'ave a wee. Will ya stop listenin'.
Josie I'm not bloody listenin'. An' I'm not gonna report 'im, I've told ya that.
But I'll see 'is mam an' dad. Why should I 'ave all the worry?

Pause. A toilet flush is heard

Kelly Leave 'er. It's 'er own fault.
Mick She's only a kid.
Kelly All right for you to say. She'll ruin this week if we let 'er.
Josie (*at the door*) Come out, babe. Come on, come out.

Silence

Come on, angel. Come out an' we'll talk.
Kim (*off*) What d' ya wanna know?
Josie Come on. We'll 'ave a ciggie an' we'll talk.
Kim (*off*) I'm not tellin' ya nothin'.
Mick Shall we get off?
Josie You stay there. It's best to 'ave a man's opinion an' all.
Kim (*off*) Is are Kelly there?
Josie Yeh.
Kim (*off*) An' Mick?
Josie We're all 'ere.

> *Silence. The bathroom door opens and Kim appears. She stands in a
> defiant manner, holding on to the bathroom door*

Kim What d' ya wanna know?
Josie I wanna know — (*Pause*) What's 'e said to ya?

Silence

Mick (*standing*) We better go.
Kim (*with haste*) 'E said, "Ya know when it's born do I 'ave to bring flowers
the 'ospital 'cos I'll feel a cunt."
Kelly (*in disbelief*) Bastard.
Josie An' that was it?
Kim Yeh.
Josie Ya better off without 'im.

Silence. Mick still stands

Mick I'm goin' the shop. Anyone want ciggies?
Josie 'Ave some a mine. I've brought plenty.
Mick I'll get some more.
Kelly Will it be open?
Josie I've got loads, Mick. You sit down an' enjoy ya 'oliday.
Mick I fancy some crisps.
Josie I've got crisps.
Mick Or chocolate or somethin'. I'll see ya later.

Mick exits

Josie 'E shouldn't go wastin' 'is money.
Kelly My money.
Josie No luck?
Kelly No jobs.
Kim There is jobs if ya look for them.
Kelly Yeh, with no money.

Kim stands at the table and starts to pick at the cake

Kim Why can't 'e work on the side like normal people?
Kelly There's nothin' goin' in 'is line a work.
Josie What is 'is line a work?
Kelly Dunno. But there's nothin' goin'.
Josie I could see if Bruce can get 'im start on the docks.
Kelly Ya must be jokin'. I wouldn't let Mick be a slave to no-one.
Josie What d'ya mean?
Kelly Bruce is at work every hour God sends. Doin' all sorts a jobs, drivin'
    all sorts a cranes. 'E doesn't even take the weekend off.
Josie Only 'cos 'e's not allowed.
Kelly Exactly. They're all forced into it.
Josie Sod the long hours, Kel. Think a the money.
Kelly I'd rather 'e signed on. I want Mick to come 'ome at the end a the day.
Josie What are you on about?
Kelly It was Bruce that said it. Long hours are dangerous.
Josie Not on that money they're not.
Kelly Me dad woulda killed you, sayin' that.
Josie Yeh. On 'is bleedin' soapbox. "Unions this, unions that." I know about
    paypackets not unions.
Kim Wish I did.
Kelly I wouldn't know what to do with meself without Mick around.
Josie Well think what ya could do with the money.

Kim I'm gonna get a nanny when I start work. She can 'ave a room in me flat at the docks an' mind it when I go clubbin'.

Josie Think you've already got a soft shite lined up for that.

Kim What?

Josie (*indicating herself*) Granny Grunt. It'll be me left 'oldin' the baby. 'Oldin' two bleedin' babies.

Kelly Yeh. I'll be paintin' the town with me Monday book.

Kim An' me with me maths books. (*Laughs*) Pushin' a pram an' carryin' me lunch box.

Kelly Givin' it "breast is best" in the middle of English.

Kim Yeh, Mave the Rave. Imagine it. 'Er mouth'd be waterin'.

Kelly At least ya could take it the playscheme with ya in the summer.

Kim Funny.

Josie Eh! You'll bring it 'ere in the summer when ——

Kim When I get ya dad's insurance.

Josie Eh! Ya won't be takin' the piss when you've got a proper 'oliday 'ome to come to.

Kelly Kim, we'll teach them Welsh an' everythin'.

Kim (*speaking Welsh*) Yackydar!

Kelly (*joining in*) Cllan — fire — perth — ging — whatever! They'll be multicultured comin' round 'ere.

Josie Ya should count ya selves lucky comin' 'ere any time. All ya'll need is ya spends an' ya petrol money for Mick. (*Pause*) An' if you want the place to yerselves, I can always stay in Bruce's caravan.

Kim When?

Josie Whenever.

Kim Who with?

Josie With Bruce.

Kim What for?

Josie I thought you'd be glad of it. Me out the way. You lot can do what ya want then.

Pause

Kim You make me sick.

Josie What did you say?

Kim You an' 'im.

Josie An' don't ya think it makes me sick?

Kim What?

Josie You. Goin' with the first one that comes along. I thought ya might 'ave been like are Kelly an' saved yerself for someone special.

Kim 'E was special.

Josie 'E's a kid.

Kim An' you're an aald slag.

Kelly Don't you talk to 'er like that.

Kim Why not? It's true. Me dad dies an' she goes with the first aald bastard that comes along. Is Bruce special?

Josie At least 'e talks to me like a person.

Kim An' me dad never?

Josie No.

Kim Ya just a liar.

Kelly Listen to you.

Kim I loved me dad an' now 'e's dead youse don't even care.

Kelly Me mum's got to live 'er life.

Kim With some dirty docker?

Josie 'E's a very nice man.

Kim What's that to me?

Josie Ya should be glad. It's down to me that you'll 'ave a permanent caravan to come to. I could easy spend the insurance on meself, ya know?

Kim I'm supposed to be grateful for a shed?

Josie Ya cheeky little bastard. You get out my sight.

Kim Don't you touch me ——

Josie I wouldn't want to ——

Kim Good. 'Cos I'm goin'.

Pause

Kelly Go on then. Give us all a bit a peace.

Silence. Kim stares

Kim goes to the door and exits, running

Told ya she'd ruin it. (*She sits on the back settee, wraps her arms round her waist and leans forward*)

Josie I'm sorry, love. I don't want 'er to spoil the week for ya. (*Pause*) She'll be back soon, right as rain. We'll all be orright. Then we'll enjoy areselves in me lovely little palace.

Pause

Kelly I've got terrible pains.

Josie Bad?

Kelly Bad enough.

Josie Inside?

Kelly Yeh. (*Pause*) Mum, get Mick.

Josie (*calling*) Kim! Kim! I won't be long, love.

Josie exits from the caravan

   Kim! Come back, love. We've got to get Mick.

Kelly lies back on the settee. She curls up, cradles herself and whimpers

SCENE 4

Garden Party

Music: "Garden Party" by Rick Nelson

The caravan. A bright evening in September 1995

Kim sits on the steps at the front of the caravan. Josie stands in the doorway behind her holding a cup of tea, wearing a cowboy hat and smoking a cigarette. Bruce, aged fifty is well-built and sexy. He believes he knows most things better than anyone else but is mellowing with age. He finds and fights for what he can. He is wearing a check shirt and western hat, and removes the "For Sale" sign from the ground. Country music can be heard being broadcast from a tannoy system throughout the scene

Josie D' ya remember that, Kim?
Kim No.
Josie Ya do. When me an' ya dad took the pensioners to Colwyn Bay. Ya must do.
Kim I don't.
Josie Anyway, they were all bleedin' paralysed drunk so when we got off the coach we 'ad to walk them 'ome. I took this one fella who lived by us an' when 'is daughter opened the door she goes, "Dad, what are you doin' 'ere?" Only turned out 'e shoulda gone back to Llandudno. 'E was stayin' with 'is wife in the convalescent 'ome. Soft sod. (*Pause*) The daughter took 'im back the next day. When they got there the mother was stiff as a board an' in a body bag. 'E's never been the same since.

Bruce lays the sign on the ground near to the caravan

Bruce Funny what a death can do.
Josie That's right. It affects people in different ways.

Bruce stands near to the door. Josie passes him the cup of tea

Bruce An' ya never know when the Lord'll take ya.
Josie Like Jimmy. Went on the chair-o-planes an' never come off. Well 'e
did come off that was the problem.
Bruce In 'is prime an' all.
Josie 'E only went on so I could get a photie, didn't 'e, Kim?
Kim I wasn't there.
Josie You weren't there, were ya? Just so everyone'd know 'e'd been on a
Spanish fair. Now no-one can forget. I didn't even manage to take the
photie, 'e was flyin' through the air before I knew what was 'appenin'. I'll
never go abroad again.
Bruce Enjoy yerself while ya can. That's my motto.
Josie Well we are.
Bruce We are.
Josie We are, aren't we, Kim?

Pause

Bruce That's 'ow Linda went an' all. Enjoyin' 'erself.
Josie The best way, I say.
Bruce 'Aydock. The two forty-five. Just as me 'orse jumped the last. She
grabbed me arm an' whoomph! — down she went. Powerful thing, strokes.
I 'ad a fiver on that 'orse an' all.
Josie Terrible that, isn't it, Kim?
Bruce She loved the gee-gees, Linda. I thought I'd never go again meself.
Josie I know nothin' about racin'.
Bruce I'll 'ave to take ya.

From inside the caravan we hear a baby crying

Josie Ooh, I'd love that. You'd like that, wouldn't ya, Kim?
Kim Is are Kelly comin' or what?
Josie Once she's finished work.
Kim Thank God for that.
Josie That's what I miss about comin' 'ere — the death page in the *Echo*.
Kim Will ya stop bein' morbid.
Bruce Someone's not 'appy.
Kim This is doin' my 'ead in.

*Kim pushes past Josie and Bruce. She enters the front bedroom of the
caravan and brings out a baby in a carry chair. In the living room, she
rocks the chair without interest*

Bruce Looks like we're in for a happy weekend.
Josie I shoulda told 'er it was country an' western.

Bruce She'll 'ave me wishin' I was back at work.

"Footsteps" by Daniel O'Donnell is now heard over the tannoy

Josie Well let's enjoy areselves while ya not.
Bruce I know. I just keep thinkin' about it.
Josie Will you cheer up an' give us kiss?

Bruce knocks Josie's hat back and kisses her. Josie breaks away

They played this at the funeral. Right at the end. We 'adn't thought about music. It didn't seem right. The priest's a big fan a Daniel O'Donnell, that's what it is. Plays 'im at weddin's an' all sorts.

Kim goes to exit the caravan

Listen what's playin'.
Kim Can I get past?

Kim pushes past and goes down the steps

Josie This was playin' at the funeral, wasn't it?
Kim No it wasn't.
Josie It was. At the end.
Kim It wasn't a funeral.
Josie Kim.
Kim It wasn't. It's not like it ever lived. It was already dead. It never died propply. It was dead when it come out an' they just put it in a dish.
Josie Ya don't mean that.
Kim I do.

The baby cries once again. Pause

I'm goin' the shop.

Kim exits

Josie Kim! Get back 'ere! (*Pause*) Come on, Kelly'll be 'ere soon!

Josie goes to enter the caravan. Bruce stands in her way and holds her

Bruce D' ya wanna stay at mine tonight?
Josie Might do.

Bruce What's that supposed to mean?
Josie Course I will. Anythin' to get away from all this.
Bruce Cheek!

Josie enters the caravan and goes to the baby

   (*Calling*) We'll go the show after, Jose. Put this strike out me 'ead an' enjoy
   areselves. What d' ya reckon?
Josie (*off*) 'Ang on. I can't find 'is dummy.
Bruce (*calling*) Raymond Froggat an' the Blue Jean Roadshow.

Josie appears from the caravan

Josie (*whispering*) Only wanted 'is dum-dum, poor little fella.

Josie walks down the steps and surveys her surroundings

Bruce 'E used to do the same clubs as me, years ago. 'E was a nice fella. Not
   that good though. Not a good crooner, like me. An' 'e couldn't get the
   women.
Josie You just wish it was you.
Bruce No I don't. If I was a star, I wouldn't know you.

Josie kisses him on the cheek

Josie It'll be a good night.
Bruce I 'ope so.
Josie They better do some Patsy Cline.
Bruce She's in the finale on Monday afternoon.
Josie Oh aye yeh!
Bruce That girl off *Stars in Their Eyes*.
Josie You'll miss it. You'll be goin' 'ome.
Bruce If there's one thing I 'ate, it's bein' on a picket first thing Monday.
Josie Stay 'ere then an' don't go.
Bruce I can't.
Josie Ya can. They won't miss ya but I will.
Bruce I'll 'ave to see.
Josie I'll make it worth ya while.
Bruce I'm sure ya will but people's livelihoods rest on this.
Josie Just stay 'ere an' 'ave a nice day.
Bruce Jose ——
Josie Eh! I could get used to this. Days off instead a stupid hours.
Bruce Don't be sayin' that, sweet'eart.

Josie Comin' up 'ere when we want. Gettin' work done on the vans. I want tubs like theirs. Two a them. One either side. An' you an' Mick can do a fence all round. I'll do the curtains. I'll do yours. I'll do them matchin'. We can rent them out then. Make a bit a money. I mean, that's what people want. Nice caravans with nice insides.

Bruce Can do that next year.

Josie Next weekend.

Bruce I'd rather I was back at work next weekend.

Josie Do ya?

Bruce Jose, we've all got to live. We're on strike, we're not on 'oliday.

Josie It's a nice idea though.

Bruce The grass is always greener, Jose.

Josie Yeh. (*Pause*) Wish Mick'd get a job.

Bruce 'E'll get one.

Josie 'E's as bad as are Kim. Tele an' tea, that's all they've got.

Bruce That'll be me before I know it.

Josie Don't be soft.

Bruce But this could be it. The bastards could just get rid.

Josie But there'll always be ships.

Bruce Yeh. An' no real dockers.

Kelly (*off*) Mum!

Josie 'Iya, love.

Kelly rushes on, breathless. She carries an Asda carrier bag

Bruce 'Allo, Kelly, darlin'.

Kelly 'Iya, Bruce.

Josie Did ya see are Kim?

Kelly She's walkin' up with Mick. 'Ow's the baby?

Josie Ah, 'e's been great.

Kelly I was dead worried. She said 'e'd been dead nowtty.

Josie She thinks it an insult if 'e snufffles, Kel.

Kelly (*gesturing the carrier bag*) I got 'im a cuddly Power Ranger.

Pause

Josie Go on in, 'e's well away.

Kelly takes a copy of the Liverpool Echo *from the bag*

Kelly I got the paper as well. (*Pause*) It's not good news, Bruce.

Bruce What's 'appened?

Kelly Looks like they've sacked all of ya. Sacked ya all.

She holds the paper out to Bruce

Bruce What does it say?
Kelly Not much. I said to Mick, "Blink an' ya'd miss it." Ya'd think it wasn't important. Should I find it?
Bruce Just tell me what it said.

Kelly starts to search through the newspaper

Kelly I think they got the P45s this mornin'.
Bruce Bastards.
Josie Yours'll be at 'ome.
Bruce I know it will.
Kelly An' I think it says the jobs 'ave already been advertised. I'll find it now.
Bruce Ya orright, Kel.
Kelly Well it's there if ya want it. (*She puts the newspaper on top of the gas canister*)
Bruce Thanks, love.
Kelly An' if there's anythin' ——
Bruce Thanks, Kel.
Kelly 'As 'e been fed?
Josie Yes, love. 'E's 'ad plenty.

Kelly enters the caravan and goes to the baby. She nurses it tenderly

Josie There's certainly no point goin' back Mondee now.
Bruce Josie, I've just lost me job. I've just lost everythin'.
Josie You'll be orright. They're bound to give it ya back. I mean, what will they do? You've worked there years.
Bruce Jose, when ya don't understand somethin', keep out of it. All right?
Josie Orright.

Pause

Bruce Promise?

He touches Josie's face

Josie You.

Josie kisses him. Loud laughter is heard offstage. Bruce looks in the direction it is coming from

Bruce No peace for the wicked.
Josie Still, it's good bein' wicked.

She kisses him again

> *Mick and Kim enter, still laughing. They carry a large holdall between them*

Kim The shame a you.
Mick Kenny Rogers an' Tammy Wynette.
Kim It suits ya that, Bruce.
Mick 'Ave to start callin' ya JR.
Josie I wish 'e 'ad 'is money.
Bruce I wish I 'ad anyone's money.
Kim Yeh. We could do with a sugar daddy, Bruce.

Mick takes two cans of beer from his holdall and offers one to Bruce

Bruce Cheers, son.
Mick No probs, bud.

Mick picks up the newspaper, flicks through it and throws it to the floor. He leans against the gas canister, takes off his shirt and takes in the sun. Bruce picks up the newspaper and sits away from the others on the grass

Josie (*to Kim*) You've perked up.
Kim Is Kelly seein' to the baby?
Josie You all right now she's 'ere?
Kim I was anyway.
Josie Well you'll 'ave to 'elp out as well.
Kim Let me enjoy meself first. Can I 'ave a can, Mick?
Josie 'Elp yerself.

Kim takes a can from his holdall

Kim We all goin' out after?
Mick Too right.
Bruce It's all the best of British tonight, if ya interested.
Mick None a that line dancin', is it?
Josie That's on tomorrow in the family bar.
Bruce Ya can count me out a that.
Mick Me an' all.
Kim An' I'm not goin'.

Josie I don't care if I go by meself.

Kim removes her T-shirt to reveal a small bikini top. Bruce opens the paper and looks through it. He pauses on a page and reads. He closes the paper, lies back and puts it behind his head

Kim I'll still be recoverin' from tonight.
Josie You're not goin' out tonight.
Kim I am.
Josie An' who's gonna mind the baby?
Kim Are Kelly.
Josie No she won't. This is 'er chance of a break.
Kim She likes stayin' in.
Josie Does she?
Kim She does, doesn't she, Mick?
Mick Sometimes, yeh.
Kim (*calling*) Kelly!
Josie Keep ya voice down.
Kim (*calling*) Kel!
Josie They're lookin' out their winda at you.
Kelly What?
Kim 'Ere a minute.

Kelly appears at the caravan door holding the baby

Kelly Keep it down. I'm just gettin' 'im off.
Kim Don't you like stayin' in?
Kelly What d' ya mean?
Kim Rather than goin' out?
Kelly Dunno ——
Kim Ya do, don't ya?
Kelly Why?
Josie 'Cos she wants you to stay in so she can go out. I've told 'er no ——
Kelly I'd rather stay in an' watch the baby.
Kim Told ya.
Kelly Is that all right then?
Kim Yeh.
Kelly All that fuss over you. Ya should see 'is little face. (*She goes down the steps*) Smile for ya mum. Go on. Smile for ya mum, not for Auntie Kelly. 'Ere she is. Ya gonna smile? Come on, mummy hold ya.

She goes to hand the baby to Kim. Kim recoils

Kim I don't want it. Put it back. I don't want it yet.

Kim sits on the step and begins to sunbathe

Kelly Go to mummy in a minute then, eh? (*She walks about nursing the baby*)
Ah, look. Look at nanny in 'er funny hat lookin' all "yee-hah". An' there's
Uncle Mick. An' Uncle Bruce. Fast asleep like you should be. Ah, poor
Uncle Bruce. (*She goes to re-enter the caravan*) Do you wanna put 'im
down, Kim?
Kim You do it.
Kelly Ya sure?
Kim Yeh.

*Kelly takes the baby into the caravan and places it back in the carry chair.
She rocks it gently*

Josie You don't know 'ow lucky you are.
Kim Don't I?
Josie 'E'll start thinkin' she's 'is mother if ya not careful.
Kim I don't care.
Josie Ya might one day.
Kim I don't wanna know.
Josie No — ya never do.

Josie lights a cigarette. Mick and Kim sunbathe. Bruce sleeps

ACT II

Scene 1

Fade Away

Music: "Fade Away" by Oasis

The caravan. A dull afternoon, March 1996

Outside the caravan are two white tubs containing flowers, two garden gnomes pulling moonies, and a plastic table and two chairs. The "For Sale" sign has now been removed completely. Inside the caravan, the soft furnishings now co-ordinate and the net curtains are whiter than white. By the door is a sealed bucket, clearly displaying the words "Support the Dockers". A radio-cassette player stands on a number of betting slips on the table

Kelly, wearing a "Support the Dockers" T-shirt, sits beside the table studying the racing page of a newspaper. She turns on the radio — a sports programme is heard. She turns it off. She takes a betting slip from her pocket and looks at it. She kisses the slip

Kelly (*slowly, relishing the words*) Encore un peu. (*She smiles, laughs softly and kisses the slip once more*)

Kim enters from the bathroom and goes to the door

Kelly swiftly places the betting slip under the radio

Kim What time does it start?
Kelly Quarter to.

Kim goes to the table and sits. She sighs

Kim Wish it'd 'urry up.
Kelly Wish I was there with them two.
Kim What one 'ave I got?
Kelly Young Hustler.
Kim Is that a good one?
Kelly Dunno. Gettin' backed though.

Kim It must be a three-legged donkey.

Kelly No. It's gone from twenty to one to fourteen to one.

Kim So do I get more money if it wins?

Kelly No, ya get less.

Kim That's not on, that.

Kelly Might 'ave a good chance though. (*Pause*) I'd love to see it live.

Kim Watch it on the tele.

Kelly I mean the atmosphere — a good day out with Bruce an' Mick, 'avin' a laugh. Instead a bein' stuck 'ere pushin' leaflets.

Kim That's not like you. You even shout "Up the dockers" in ya sleep.

Kelly I'm not gettin' bored of it. It would 'ave been a good day out that's all.

Kim Listen to you. Never thought you'd be into dockers an' 'orses.

Kelly It's good.

Kim What is? Picket lines an' 'orse manure? You've gone weird, Kel.

Kelly Don't be soft.

Kim Ya 'ave. I mean, look at today. Ya palm are baby off on to me mum so ya can listen to a 'orse race an' shake a bucket for the dockers in the family bar. Now that's weird.

Kelly No, it's not. Things change.

Kim Yeh, they might a bit. But not like you. It's a wonder Mick puts up with ya.

Kelly Don't worry. 'E doesn't.

Kim What?

Kelly 'E's seein' someone else.

Kim No.

Kelly 'E is.

Kim 'As 'e told ya?

Kelly Doesn't 'ave to.

Kim Well 'ow d'ya know?

Kelly 'Cos 'e's been doin' sit-ups.

Kim Go 'way. Are ya gonna find out who it is an' knock 'er 'ead off?

Kelly reads the racing pages

Kelly Got more important things to think about.

Kim So what are ya gonna do?

Kelly Nothin'.

Kim 'Ow come? D' ya wanna get shut?

Kelly I only married 'im 'cos of the baby.

Kim The photos were nice though. It wasn't a complete waste of time. (*Pause*) 'Ave ya got any idea who it could be?

Kelly I thinks it's someone from the job club.

Kim No.

Kelly Well 'e's been signin' on for years. All of a sudden goes the job club an' can't get enough of it. What does that say to you?

Kim Doesn't say anythin'.

Kelly Course it does. 'E's joined just to get a bit of extra fanny.

Kim 'E might be tryin' to get a job.

Kelly Mick's 'appy to live on 'andouts an' my Asda ten per cent discount.

Kim P'raps 'e wants to save up. Change 'is life a bit.

Kelly 'E buys scratch cards for that.

Kim I think you're over-reactin'.

Kelly Kim, 'e wears *Escape For Men* whenever 'e goes. Now what does that say?

Kim That 'e wants to smell nice.

Kelly Come off it.

Kim 'E might be just tryin'.

Kelly Tryin' it on. Anyway d'ya think I'm bothered? She can 'ave 'im, the lazy get. I shouldn't 'ave let 'im near me in the first place.

Kim Will ya kick 'im out me mum's?

Kelly When I find out who she is.

Kim I thought ya weren't bothered?

Kelly I'm not 'avin some scrubber takin' me 'usband just like that. There'll 'ave to be a fight first ——

Kim A proper fight?

Kelly Then she can 'ave 'im. The sly bastard.

Kim Kelly, ya don't wanna 'ave loads of upset again. Ya should leave it. Let Mick sort it out 'imself.

Pause

Kelly Ya don't think it's someone from the pub, do ya?

Kim No. Why?

Kelly It's just that sometimes 'e 'as a smell on 'im. Ya know a smell that ya know but ya don't know why?

Kim It's probably 'is aftershave.

Kelly Not that kind a smell. Not a perfume smell, a person smell. The smell a clothes, the smell of skin. A person smell. A smell that ya know but ya can't think why ——

Kim turns on the radio. From the commentary, we hear that the race is in its closing stages. The commentary continues through the rest of the scene

Kim Kelly, ya missin' ya race.

Kelly I really know it. (*Slight pause*) An' don't forget you owe Bruce for ya bet.

Kim I know, fifty pence.

Kelly A pound plus tax. Mine's just got a mention. That's one pound ten.

Kim Young Hustler. That's mine.

Kelly A pound bet an' ten pence for ya tax.

Kim I don't pay tax.

Kelly Ya do in the bettin' shop.

Kim Robbin' bastards.

Kelly Who was that?

Kim Lord somethin' an' somethin' else.

Kelly Not one of ares. (*Pause*) When I went to Haydock, Bruce said that
whatever wins there — that's us. Imagine if it's first an' second! I can still
smell that ——

Kim Come on, Hustler. Hustle ya bastard.

Kelly Top weight. Yours 'as 'ad it.

Kim Ya know that smell, what's it like?

Kelly Like — like — I can smell it now. Right under me nose. Like I can
never get away from it. Go on, Encore!

Kim What if it's someone ya know?

Kelly I'll kill them.

*Kelly turns up the radio. The following two speeches overlap along with the
radio commentary*

Come on, Encore! Don't drop back. Come on for Godsake — ya can win
this — listen to that — come on, come 'ead. Come on, my son! — Fuck
off, Rough Quest — ooh, bloody 'alf — ya lazy get — ya nearly there —
Go 'ead, lad — run — run, ya bastard — 'e's in front! It's gonna win! Come
on, Encore — come on. Can ya believe that? Can ya believe it?

Kim (*very quietly*) Kel, ya know them, Kel. Ya must do. Ya must know. You
must know who it is. Not that I wanna hurt ya, I don't. I don't want ya to
be upset again. Not after the baby. It 'appened before you. Then it 'appened
again. An' now it's like I can't 'elp meself. I've got what I wanted an' that's
hard to let go. Rough Quest? Mick's got a fiver on Rough Quest.

The race has come to an end. Kelly turns down the radio

Kelly What did ya say?

Kim Mick's won. 'E 'ad a fiver on Rough Quest.

Kelly Typical. 'Im first, me second.

Kim An' I'm third.

Kelly In a photo.

Kim Ya never know.

Kelly Bruce 'ad Superior Finish in the sweep.

Kim I 'ope mine beats 'is.
Kelly Me mum's never even got a mention.
Kim I 'ate losin' to someone who knows it all.
Kelly Ya like Mick. Always 'ave to be the winner.

Kelly turns off the radio, as the commentary announces there is to be a stewards' inquiry. She reaches inside the caravan door and picks up the sealed bucket

Kim An' 'e is.
Kelly But not without a fight. I'll 'ave to go an' shake me bucket. See ya.

Kelly exits

Pause. Kim takes the betting slips from under the radio, looks at them and puts them back. She turns on the radio as Rough Quest is announced the winner. She takes a betting slip from her pocket and kisses it

Kim (*triumphantly*) Rough bloody Quest!

SCENE 2

I Just Don't Know What To Do With Myself

Music: "I Just Don't Know What To Do With Myself" by Dusty Springfield

The caravan, the following morning

Josie, wearing a dressing-gown, sits on the back settee with a large cardboard box at her side. Kelly sits in front of her on the floor. She stacks leaflets all around her and then counts the contents of each pile

Josie What about these?
Kelly (*as she counts*) What?
Josie "Ten things they never wanted you to know about our docks."
Kelly (*in between counting*) I'm not takin' them.
Josie Why not?
Kelly (*she loses count*) Everyone binned them yesterday. No-one's interested.
Josie I think they're good.

Kim enters from the bathroom carrying a make-up bag. Her hair is wrapped in a towel. She sits at the table and begins to make herself up

Kelly Bruce said they're too factual for 'olidaymakers. 'E was right.
Josie I don't think so, d'you, Kim?
Kim What?

Josie picks up a handful of leaflets and shows them to Kim

Josie These ones.
Kelly I was countin' them.
Kim Dunno. Never read it.
Kelly We're not takin' them anyway.
Josie We should take whatever we can. Everyone passes through that bar at
    dinnertime.
Kelly I would if we were sellin' them.

She hands Josie a pile of leaflets

    Ee are, take them.
Josie These new?
Kelly Yeh.
Josie (*reading*) "Stand by our Men." Who wrote these?
Kim Tammy Wynette.
Josie (*she reads*) Ooh, I don't like this. "We even sent the director a birthday
    cake. It was a sign of good will, a peace offering, an olive branch" —
    sounds like Jesus — "Even so we made sure that the cake wasn't a very nice
    one." (*She looks up*) I got that cake. Not very nice? Bleedin' cheek. Who
    wrote that?
Kelly Me.
Kim Ya make them sound like Palestines.
Josie Ya coulda put it better than that. Like — "But we 'ad to get a cheap one
    'cos we was skint."
Kelly But we didn't want the bastard to 'ave a nice one.
Kim Yers shoulda got 'im a doughnut.
Kelly Yeh. Or an ice bun.
Kim (*laughing*) Imagine an ice bun stickin' through ya letter-box.
Kelly You'd know there was gonna be trouble.
Josie (*laughing*) Or you'd think it was your lucky day.
Kelly Speak for yerself.
Kim Aye. I'm gonna tell Bruce that ya think 'e's got a thing like a crusty
    bun——
Josie But you shouldn't be writing this, Kelly.
Kelly Why?
Josie 'Cos Mick's on the dole not the docks.
Kelly So?

Josie It's not your place.

Kelly It's no-one's place. It's support. (*She stands and begins to put the leaflets into the box*) I don't see you writin' anythin' for Bruce.

Josie That's not the point.

Kelly Yeh it is.

Josie Some women's 'usbands 'ave worked there thirty-odd years. I've known Bruce five minutes ——

Kim Eighteen months.

Josie — an' you think ya can go along an' throw yerself in. Writing all sorts, doin' raffles. Yer never at 'ome.

Kelly checks through the box and closes it

Kelly Is that it? Ya bothered that I'm never at 'ome?

Josie You'll be treadin' on people's toes.

Kelly Are ya?

Josie picks up the last pile of leaflets, "Ten things …" from the floor

Josie What about these?

Kim Can I lend your 'airdryer?

Kelly I'm not takin' them. Yeh, it's in me mum's room.

Kim It's took me that long to do me nails. It's gonna look crap now.

Kim exits to Josie's bedroom

Kelly They're just glad of the 'elp. No matter who it is.

Josie That's what they say.

Kelly picks up papers from the floor and goes to the table

Kelly Ya should do a bit yerself.

Josie I do. I bought the cake.

Kelly You just go to work an' come 'ome again.

Josie Well that's enough. Anyway what d'ya think I'm doin' 'ere?

Kelly You're on 'oliday.

Josie I'm 'elpin' you.

Kelly Sittin' there?

Josie I sit on the stall. I do the raffle.

Kelly An' stay today. No slippin' the bingo.

The sound of a hairdryer in Josie's room can be heard

Josie But Lady Muck gets away with it?

Kelly She's not interested.
Josie Might give 'er somethin' to do.
Kelly Couldn't 'ave the baby there. He's into everythin'.
Josie I'd mind 'im.
Kelly Did I give you that list a raffle prizes?
Josie It's in the box.
Kelly I've got that many lists.

The hairdryer stops

Josie 'Ope I win that whisky.
Kelly We can't buy tickets.
Josie Why?
Kelly 'Cos we're runnin' it.

Kim emerges from the bedroom with partly dried hair

Kim Bloody lecky's gone.
Josie You'll 'ave to go the office.
Kim I'm gonna be late now.
Josie An 'urry up 'cos a the fridge.
Kim The shame a this. I 'ope no-one sees me.

Kim steps out of the front door and looks about. She exits hurriedly. Kelly uses the interruption to revise her lists. She concentrates on her paperwork throughout the following dialogue. Josie lights a cigarette. Silence

Josie But I could just buy one. It's not like anyone'd know?
Kelly I would.
Josie I only wanna win it for Bruce.
Kelly Bruce donated it.
Josie 'E what? 'As it got a funny name?
Kelly Somethin' Scottish.
Josie Yeh. I got 'im that. The cheeky bastard. Where is it?
Kelly It's in the back of the car.
Josie (*standing*) I'll 'ave that. Where's ya keys?
Kelly Ya can't take it.
Josie It's my whisky.
Kelly It's for the raffle.
Josie No-one'll know. Just cross it off ya list.
Kelly It's raisin' money for people to live off.
Josie A bottle a whisky? Talk sense.
Kelly The list's typed up now.

Josie Givin' away bleedin' presents.

Kim runs on and enters the caravan. She is in a rush

Kim It's freezin' out there. I was gonna wear me satin A-line an' all.
Josie Ya know that whisky I got for Bruce?

Kim picks up a mirror from the table and finishes her make-up

Kim Off that fella in the *Barley Mow*?
Josie 'E's only give it in for the raffle.
Kelly No wonder if some tealeaf's sellin' it in a pub. It's probably rank.
Kim It is.
Josie An' 'ow do you know?
Kim I 'ad some.
Kelly So the bottle's 'alf empty?
Kim No. Me an' Mick 'ad a drink in the *Barley Mow* after we'd been the dole an' Mick bought some off some fella. We 'ad some watchin' "Blossoms in the Dust". That's a brilliant film. It's black an' white but it's dead good ——
Kelly Mick bought some?
Kim Yeh but we threw it away.
Kelly An' 'e moans about money. I could kill 'im. Sittin' on 'is arse. That coulda been another raffle prize, that.
Josie (*to herself*) Cheeky bastard.

Kim puts down the mirror and make-up. She makes her way towards Josie's bedroom

Kim All men are bastards.
Josie Whoever said that knew what they were on about.
Kim Course they did. They were probbly a lezzy.

Kim exits into Josie's bedroom

Pause

Josie That's really hurt me, that 'as.
Kelly Praps 'e doesn't like whisky.
Josie 'E doesn't like somethin', the belchin' bastard. 'E's out every chance 'e gets.

The sound of the hairdryer is heard once more

Kelly Only 'cos a the dispute.
Josie "I'm goin' to HQ, I can't come round." 'E's out as much as you are.
Kelly 'E 'as to be. 'E's a leadin' man.
Josie Leadin' someone else, that's for sure.

Kelly stands and picks up her paperwork

Kelly Are you gonna moan all day?
Josie No.
Kelly Come on, I need ya to 'elp me set up.
Josie (*snapping*) Me whole life revolves around this bleedin' strike.
Kelly 'Ow d' ya think I feel?
Josie That's out a choice. I 'ad somethin' goin' with Bruce till all this started.
 Now 'e's out gallivantin' everywhere with God knows who.
Kelly Don't be stupid.
Josie Well 'e's gettin' it somewhere 'cos 'e's not gettin' it from me.
Kelly Like who?
Josie Like someone.
Kelly Like who?
Josie Someone. Someone at these conferences.

Pause. The sound of the hairdryer stops

Like someone at your women's group.

Silence

Kelly I don't know where ya get ya ideas from 'cos they're not from the same
 place as mine.
Josie No, yours are from the same place as Bruce's.
Kelly P'raps you shoulda got involved from the start ——
Josie Imagine me? Thick as two short planks.
Kelly Instead a bein' pathetic an' twisted. You coulda gone on conferences
 an' weekends ——
Josie Someone 'as to cook the tea.
Kelly Don't get at me. If I'm not there Mick should do 'is own.
Kim (*off*) Kel?
Kelly (*quietly, indicating the bedroom*) An' she should pull 'er weight an'
 all. (*She picks up the box*)

*Kim appears from Josie's room. She is dressed in a short, satin A-line skirt
and carries a pair of bright, strappy shoes*

Kim When are ya goin', Kel?
Kelly Now.
Kim Take us up the nursery. I'm gonna be late.
Kelly So am I.
Josie Bleedin' whisky, cheeky get.
Kelly Are you comin' or what?

Kim sits at the table and puts on her shoes

Josie I'm gonna 'ave to 'ave the day off today. All that whisky business 'as
gone to me 'ead. Ya don't mind do ya, Kel?
Kelly Ya just not interested. An' that's that.
Kim I 'ope it doesn't rain on me way back. These'll be ruined.
Josie Ya don't mind do ya?
Kelly (*smiling*) Only if I can raffle ya bingo prizes.
Kim I looked a meff when I took 'im, I don't wanna look a meff when I pick
'im up.
Josie Soddin' whisky, cheeky bugger.

Kelly goes down the caravan steps carrying the box, Kim follows

Kelly I'll see ya after.
Kim I mean, ya never know who ya meet pushin' a pram, do ya?

They exit

Josie sits with her head in her hands. She sighs and looks up

Josie Fuckin' whisky, bleedin' bastard.

SCENE 3

Promises Promises

Music: "Promises, Promises" by Dionne Warwick

The caravan. A bright summer Tuesday, 1996

*Bruce sits outside the caravan with his shirt off and his feet on the plastic
table. He reads the Mirror. Josie stands next to the table wearing her
dressing-gown and sunglasses. She unpacks a freezer-bag on to the table. Its
contents consist of food parcelled in foil and a Thermos flask*

Josie So I told 'er. 'Ow was I supposed to know that Thermos flasks explode
at thirty thousand feet? It doesn't say nothin' in the brochures. I only took
it in case there was nowhere open when we got there. She just looked at me.
Cheeky bitch. She should've stuck to sellin' Estay fuckin' Lauder.

*She takes a baby's dummy from the bag and puts it on the table. She repacks
the food*

So never take a Thermos on a plane. Not full anyway. Ya can take one
empty. Or 'alf full. Depends 'ow hot it is. That's 'ow they break, ya see.
They get to a point when they get too hot an' that's it. They crack. Well
some of them do. There are flasks an' flasks. I've always preferred a
Thermos meself. (*She picks up the flask and tries to squeeze it into the bag*)
You should take one on the line with ya.

Bruce I'd never get round to makin' it that time a the mornin'.

Josie (*fastening the bag*) Funny, isn't it? 'Ow do they know to keep hot things
hot an' cold things cold.

Bruce (*playing her along*) Like Japanese radios. It's great 'ow they all talk
English.

Josie Oh yeh. I never thought of that.

She goes to enter the caravan

When ya think about it, they've got a bleedin' cheek them air 'ostesses.
They think they're somethin' when they're not. They're no different from
me workin' on school dinners. I mean the only difference is that their
canteen flies.

She enters the caravan and goes into her bedroom

*Bruce opens the freezer-bag and takes out a large parcel. He unwraps it and
takes out a cheese sandwich*

*Kim enters from the bathroom. She wears a swimming costume, shorts,
and fake tan and carries an inexpensive women's magazine. She goes
outside*

Kim 'Iya, Bruce.

Bruce Mornin' love.

Kim (*picking up the dummy from the table and wiping the teat*) What's she
like? It'll 'ave all shite on it now. (*She puts the dummy in her mouth and
sucks hard. She takes it out and looks at it*) Better. (*She sits down and starts
to read the magazine*) Bruce?

Bruce Yeh?

Kim I've just 'ad this terrible dream about you. You were in it but ya died. Ya were walkin' back to your caravan right, an' ya just walked into this pane a glass. It never smashed or nothin'. Ya just walked into it, banged ya 'ead an' died.

Bruce Thanks for brightenin' me day.

Kim Me mum was dead upset. An' she invited loadsa people to the funeral like it was weddin' or somethin'. It was dead weird.

Bruce You'll 'ave to find out what it means from one of them books.

Kim It wasn't like me dad's funeral. I cried me eyes out at that. In this one I just sat there dead still.

Bruce It all means somethin'.

Kim I know yeh. Like when me dad died I used to dream about 'im every night for ages. Suppose that's 'cos I missed 'im.

Bruce I still dream about Linda.

Kim Is that 'cos ya miss 'er?

Bruce I think about 'er. But don't tell ya mam.

Kim I think about me dad. But I miss 'im more than I think about 'im. (*Pause*) Ya don't mind me sayin' that, do ya?

Bruce No. Ya dad's ya dad.

Kim Mm. Jimmy.

Bruce An' I suppose you're the kid I never 'ad.

Kim An' Kelly.

Bruce Well — yeh. Yeh, ya right.

Kim Just think, Bruce. If you married me mum, we would be.

Bruce Oh aye yeh.

Kim But I wouldn't call ya Dad. I'd call ya Bruce.

Josie enters from her bedroom. She wears shorts, a T-shirt and has her sunglasses on her head

Bruce I wouldn't expect ya to.

Josie To what?

Kim I was just sayin' that if you got married to Bruce then 'e'd be like are dad an' we'd be 'is kids. But I wouldn't call 'im Dad, I'd call 'im Bruce.

Bruce An' I said I wouldn't expect 'er to.

Kim But the baby could call ya Grandad 'cos 'e wouldn't know no difference.

Josie I'm glad to see you've sorted are lives out.

Kim I just meant if ya did.

Bruce She sounds keen though, doesn't she, Jose?

Josie (*laughing*) I would've bin keen meself if ya 'adn't a started on me butties.

Bruce Well don't go worryin'. I can't see the support committee givin' us
a sub for a weddin' when Seldom Seen's got a repossession order.
Kim Who?
Bruce Seldom Seen — 'e was always off sick.
Josie Don't put the dummy in ya mouth, Kim. It's unhygienic.
Kim It's my baby.
Josie Sometimes I wonder.

Josie takes the dummy from Kim and picks up the bag. Kim resumes reading

An' make sure ya follow me down. Are Kelly was up at the crack a dawn
with 'im.
Kim I will.
Josie I'll see ya later.
Bruce D'ya want ya butties?
Josie No, you 'ave them. Token a my love. Ta-ra.

Josie exits

Bruce See ya, hon.
Kim Ta-ra. (*Pause*) Ya know that Sneldon? Is that 'is real name?
Bruce Who?
Kim Sneldon.
Bruce Seldom. No, it's a nickname.
Kim Oh.
Bruce We all 'ave nicknames.
Kim Do ya? What like?
Bruce All sorts. Cinderella, Dicky Twice, Enno, Skippy ——
Kim So why's that fella called Seldom Seen?
Bruce I told ya. 'Cos 'e's always off.
Kim An' what's 'is real name?
Bruce (*laughs*) Dunno. Never seen 'im to ask.
Kim But why?
Bruce 'Cos 'e was always on the sick.
Kim No. Why the names?
Bruce Tradition. You've got to 'ave tradition in a place like the docks
otherwise what's the point? Mind you, what is the point? Look at me. I used
to be on me break at this time an' now I'm sittin' 'ere doin' nothin'. It's
tradition they're takin' away. That an' decent conditions. Not to mention
'undreds of jobs an' a way of life. A city's way of life. A bloody river's way
of life. A decent retirement for fellas like me ——
Kim An' what do they call you?
Bruce Me? "The man with the mouth."

Kim 'Cos you do all the talkin'.

Bruce Yeh.

Kim Well ya know that Cinderella bloke? Was 'e gay?

Bruce No. 'E just always 'ad to be in for midnight.

Kim That's good that. What about the others? What were they again?

Bruce Erm. Right. (*Quickly*) Cinderella — I've gorra be in for midnight, Dicky Twice — 'is name is Richard Richards, Enno 'cos 'e's a tight arse, "Dad, can I 'ave an ice-cream?" N — O, NO — "Arthur, can I borrow ya tools?" N — O, NO. Someone wrote them all down once. A big list. Don't know what 'appened to that.

Kim They're good them. Like somethin' out the *Viz*.

Bruce An' soon to be a thing a the past, Kim.

Kim Yeh. It's gone crap, 'asn't it? I only like the Fat Slags.

Pause. Kim turns over a page and starts to read

Bruce D'you know who is it we're fightin', Kim?

Kim Who's fightin'?

Bruce D'you know what your Kelly's doin' the campaignin' for?

Kim For money for the dockers.

Bruce Yeh. But d'ya know about the principles? D'ya know what caused it?

Kim Yeh. Ya all got sacked 'cos they want young fellas there who can do more work.

Bruce They want young fellas so they can pay them a pittance an' 'ave them workin' like casuals. Kim, we were the most productive workforce in Europe. Young or not, they can't do more work than we did.

Kim They can probbly do it for longer though.

Bruce At what price?

Kim Well it'd be more than the dole.

Bruce I mean safety. I mean lives.

Pause

Kim D'ya get paid if ya a scab?

Bruce Yeh.

Kim That's all right, isn't it?

Bruce No. No, it's not.

Kim But someone's got to do the work.

Kelly enters. She is out of breath

Bruce Yeh — dockers 'ave. Trained men. Docks are dangerous places, it's a skilled job.

Kelly They are if ya a scab. Scuse me.

Kelly runs in to the caravan and enters the bathroom

Bruce Right. The thing is, Kim. It's wrong to take another person's job. Right?
Kim Yeh.
Bruce Especially if that person had been doin' that same job for say twenty-odd years? Right?
Kim Yeh.
Bruce An' that person 'ad been stopped from doin' his job because they were sacked for bein' on strike. Right?
Kim Yeh.
Bruce So that's it. We want are jobs back. We want the same rights as what other people 'ave got. Otherwise we're gonna be back in the dark ages. Now d'ya understand?
Kim Yeh.
Bruce Good girl.

Pause. Kim reads

Kim Ya know what it's all down to, don't ya?
Bruce What?
Kim The ozone layer.
Bruce What is?

A toilet flush is heard

Kim The dark ages. Ya wanna read the label on ya deodorant an' use a ice bucket instead of a fridge.
Bruce (*despairing*) So that's the reason. I'll 'ave to tell the lads. (*He resumes reading his paper*)

Kelly emerges from the bathroom. She hitches up her skirt slightly and goes out of the caravan

Kelly Never thought I'd make it. Them toilets by the beach are rank.
Bruce Should 'ave gone in the sea.
Kelly I know ——
Kim Eeh! Would you wee in the sea?
Kelly No ——
Bruce That's where it goes anyway.
Kelly But I would if I was desperate.

Kelly sits on the arm of Bruce's chair

Kim That's disgustin'.
Kelly You've done worse.
Kim I 'aven't.
Kelly You 'ave. You pissed in the sand in Abersoch.
Kim I never.
Kelly Ya did. I remember ya doin' it.
Bruce It's all comin' out now, Kim.
Kelly She even said she wanted to do it again.
Kim No I never.
Bruce She's goin' red.
Kim I was about three.
Kelly Ya were eight.
Kim At least I wouldn't do it now. Ya should 'ave respect for nature.
Kelly So should you. I believe fake tan causes terrible scum in the sea.
Kim This is my natural colour.
Kelly What? Orange.
Kim At least I look attractive.
Kelly Ya might do to a scally.
Kim What's wrong with scallies?
Kelly (*laughs*) In a word? Mick.
Kim What are ya sayin' that to me for?
Kelly 'Cos ya asked.
Kim You're dead tight on 'im.
Kelly Tight? 'E's lived off me since I met 'im.
Kim You don't give 'im a chance.
Kelly I've give 'im plenty. Just that I'm fed up a livin' with someone who doesn't give a shit about nothin'.
Kim At least 'e's tryin'.
Kelly This is the first interview 'e's ever gone to.
Kim You'll even be moanin' if 'e gets the job, you. What's up, found someone else?
Kelly No ——
Bruce She deserves better, that's all.
Kelly I just don't wanna work on a till all me life.
Kim State a you.
Bruce Kelly's got ambitions.
Kim So 'ave I.
Bruce An' what do you want?
Kim I want me own business.
Kelly Doin' what?
Kim I dunno. Just a business.

Bruce So ya shouldn't knock Kelly for wantin' to get on in life.
Kim OK.
Bruce 'Cos no-one should get knocked for doin' that.
Kim Orright. I get the message. (*She stands and takes some sandwiches from the parcel*)
Kelly If Mick gets this job we're gonna get a mortgage.
Kim Can I 'ave these? Ya get 'ungry by the sea.
Bruce Yeh.
Kim I knew you'd go all snobby.
Kelly It's not snobby, it's sensible. Plannin' for the future.
Kim Whatever turns ya on. I'll see ya after.
Bruce See ya, love.

Kim exits

Kelly She does my 'ead in. I always thinks she knows. (*She sits on the table*)
Bruce 'Ow would she know?
Kelly 'Cos she's always gettin' at me.
Bruce Well ya can't let 'er spoil it.

Pause

Kelly Nothin' gets to you, does it?
Bruce Some things do.
Kelly Like what?

Pause

Bruce Ya not gonna get a house with 'im, are ya?
Kelly What?
Bruce A mortgage?
Kelly I might do.
Bruce So much for us then.
Kelly Well you've practically moved into ares.
Bruce Only so I can see you.
Kelly Not me mum?
Bruce Well what can I do? If I lose ya mum, I lose you. You told me that.
Kelly She is me mum, Bruce.
Bruce An' I'm doin' me best not to ruin everythin' you've got.

Pause

Kelly D' ya sleep with 'er?

Bruce Kelly.
Kelly Do ya?
Bruce When I 'ave to.
Kelly D' ya enjoy it?
Bruce No.
Kelly Does she?

Pause

Bruce Yeh.
Kelly I knew she did. Sometimes I 'ear ya. I never used to 'ear 'er an' me dad.
Bruce That's 'cos ya listenin' out for it.

Kelly stands

Kelly That's 'cos I can't 'elp 'earin'.
Bruce Why d'ya think we stay at my van? I do think about ya.
Kelly While ya doin' it? Thanks.

Kelly enters the caravan

Bruce I think about ya all the time.

Bruce follows her inside with the sandwiches. He shuts the door behind him

Kelly Even when ya with 'er?
Bruce Yeh. Do you?

Pause

Kelly Yeh.
Bruce So ya 'ave sex with 'im?
Kelly Yeh.
Bruce Why?
Kelly I just do.
Bruce An' ya like it?
Kelly No. I turn me 'ead away.
Bruce So why are ya gonna stay with 'im?
Kelly I'm twenty years of age.
Bruce You said that made no difference.
Kelly Between us, it doesn't. It's just everyone else.
Bruce An' that's it?
Kelly I don't like it, ya know. I don't like any of it.

Bruce So what are ya gonna do?

Kelly I don't know. What are you gonna do? (*Pause*) Stay at ares with me mum? Stay at your caravan with me mum?

Bruce It's not what I want.

Kelly What do ya want?

Bruce Somethin' different. Why? What do you want?

Kelly I don't want Mick.

Bruce So what do we do?

Kelly (*shrugs*) I don't know. Life goes on.

Bruce touches her face. They embrace and kiss. Kelly takes his hand

   They exit to Josie's bedroom

SCENE 4

Sticks and Stones

Music: "Sticks and Stones" by Donna Fargo

The caravan, the following evening

Kelly, now wearing a light cardigan, is in the kitchen area. She takes cutlery and two plates from a cupboard and places them on the table. She sits on the bench facing forward

Mick enters. He carries two parcels of chips. As he enters the caravan Kelly stands and approaches him. She takes the parcels from him, unwraps one of them and puts the contents — fishcake and chips — on to a plate

Kelly You were quick.

Mick I ran.

Kelly Did ya 'ave enough?

Mick Just. Yeh.

Kelly Least they're hot.

Mick Yeh.

Kelly I'm bloody starvin'. Never 'ad no dinner.

Mick 'Ow come?

Kelly Thought I'd wait for you. Me stomach thinks me throat's bin cut.

Mick Ya never 'ad to.

Kelly I'm just sayin' I'm 'ungry.

Mick Not rubbin' it in that I got 'ere late?

Kelly No.

Mick Sounds like it, an' all. I get an interview for the first time in fuckin'
years an' you 'ave to start kickin' off 'cos things run a bit late.
Kelly I said I was hungry. End a story. Ee are.

*She pushes a plate towards Mick. He sits at the table and begins to eat. She
begins to unwrap the other parcel*

But it went all right?
Mick Not bad. 'Ave ya got any sauce?
Kelly There's nothin' in. Not even bread.
Mick Fuckin' disgustin' dry chips.
Kelly Did they seem to like ya or what?
Mick Dunno. Doesn't matter, does it, whether they like ya or not? It's a job.
They just wanna know if ya can do it.
Kelly 'Ow come ya got me fishcake? Ya know I 'ate it. Bleedin' waste a
money.
Mick I'll eat it, you can 'ave me chips. End a story.

Mick swaps her fishcake for a small amount of his chips

Kelly (*with irony*) Easy on the chips, Mick.

He adds a few more chips

Didn't they 'ave no cod?
Mick There's cod in these. Just that they're round.
Kelly Shite a cod, ya mean. It's just mushed-up fish.
Mick Fish is a rip-off, anyway.
Kelly I would a give ya money if ya didn't 'ave enough.

She sits next to Mick and starts to eat

Ya shoulda said. Ya usually do.
Mick I 'ad to get ciggies. I forgot.
Kelly You need nicotine more than I need nutrients? God, just eatin' chips
must be so for bad for ya ——
Mick Will you stop moanin'?
Kelly I've got a right to moan. I sent ya for fish an' chips ——
Mick I've bin tryin' to get a fuckin' job to keep you fuckin' 'appy. I coulda
just stayed at 'ome an' not bothered with the fuckin' family 'oliday ——
Kelly I wish ya 'ad.
Mick I wish I fuckin' 'ad.

Kelly Ya might as well a done. You don't tell me nothin' anyway. What's it for? The Secret Service?

Mick Give it a rest.

Kelly See. Ya can't even 'ave a conversation. I am tryin' ya know? I am interested.

Mick It was orright.

Kelly An' 'ow all right's orright'? Is it good orright, bad orright, shite orright? What?

Mick Just orright, really.

Kelly So ya never got it?

Mick No.

Kelly "No" ya never got it?

Mick No.

Kelly So ya didn't *not* get it?

Mick Yeh ——

Kelly So ya got it?

Mick Yeh ——

Kelly Did ya?

Mick That's what I said.

Kelly Why didn't ya say?

Mick I did.

Kelly I don't understand you. Ya should be made up. When d' ya start?

Mick Mondee, I think.

Kelly And?

Mick Eight o'clock.

Kelly An' what are you doin'? What is it? Where is it? 'Ow much?

Mick It's in town an' there's quite a bit of overtime.

Kelly A factory or a site or what?

Mick Labourin'.

Kelly On a site?

Mick No.

Kelly Where?

Mick On the docks.

Pause

Kelly No.

Mick Not the same docks as where Bruce was. It's a got a different name.

Kelly Course it's the same dock. I mean ya not talkin' about the Albert Dock, are ya?

Mick Well ya wouldn't catch me workin' in a art gallery.

Kelly So you're gonna work on the docks as a docker?

Mick A dock labourer ——

Kelly You're gonna be a fuckin' scab?
Mick It's four pound an hour.

Kelly stands

Kelly I don't believe this ——
Mick It was you who wanted me to get a job.
Kelly Not like that ——
Mick It's you who wants a house ——
Kelly A house? A scabby 'ouse with a scabby 'usband? With paint on ya door an' bars on ya windas?
Mick It's a start.
Kelly I'm on the women's committee, for God's sake. My 'usband can't turn into scab labour.
Mick That's your trouble. Ya think you're so fuckin' clever with ya women's group an' ya meetin's an' committees. Praps ya should pay attention to what really matters. Like me ——
Kelly Fuck off.
Mick Don't you fuckin' tell me to fuck off. (*He knocks Kelly's plate to the floor*) Ya fuckin' moanin' bastard.
Kelly Don't start, Mick ——

He knocks the other plate to the floor

Mick I 'aven't started.
Kelly Pick that up.
Mick No.
Kelly Pick it up.
Mick That's your job.
Kelly Like providin' for me's yours? 'Cos ya 'aven't stuck to that part a the bargain, 'ave ya?
Mick Go on, rub it in me face.
Kelly An' what's Bruce gonna say?
Mick It's got nothin' to do with Bruce. This is me an' you.
Kelly Course it's got somethin' to do with Bruce. 'E's a docker.
Mick Sometimes I wonder why you're so interested.
Kelly Don't talk soft. All I care about is stoppin' scum like you from 'elpin' themselves ——
Mick Ya think I'm scum 'cos I'm 'elpin' meself?
Kelly To other people's jobs ——
Mick I'm only doin' it for you!
Kelly Suppose there's always a first time.
Mick You wanted us to do things propply.

Kelly begins to pick up the debris from the floor. She does this slowly throughout the dialogue, often stopping completely

Kelly Is that what I said? I must want me 'ead testin' ——
Mick An' now we've got a chance to get somewhere, ya don't wanna know——
Kelly I don't wanna know ——
Mick D' ya wanna live in ya mam's all ya life, is that?
Kelly I'd rather that. I'd rather that than be stuck with you for forty years —
Mick So you'd rather I went?
Kelly Do what ya want.
Mick Ya wanna get rid a me?
Kelly Never wanted ya in the first place.
Mick I knew this 'd 'appen.
Kelly I wish I'd just met ya on 'oliday an' left it at that ——
Mick Ya can't do this, Kelly ——
Kelly I mean, it was a waste a time gettin' married ——
Mick Just 'cos of a job on the docks ——
Kelly I only did it 'cos a the baby an' look what 'appened to that ——
Mick Ya can't throw it away ——
Kelly I shoulda threw it away long ago.
Mick But ya can't ——
Kelly Why not?
Mick Ya can't say that to me now ——
Kelly Mick, I don't want ya. An' I certainly don't want ya now ya messin' up people's lives.
Mick An' what about mine?
Kelly Never realized you 'ad one.
Mick Ya can't just let this go, Kelly.
Kelly I should 'ave 'ad more sense in the first place.
Mick You're tellin' me I've been wastin' my life?
Kelly I've been wastin' mine. Married to scum. What about ya bit a stuff, eh? Can't ya sniff round that?
Mick What are ya talkin' about?
Kelly You know quite well. Won't ya get what ya want off 'er? Or won't she bail ya out like I do?
Mick I don't know what ya on about.
Kelly Come off it. Ya obviously 'aven't fancied me for ages.
Mick If I wanted someone else I woulda gone ages ago.
Kelly What's up? Frightened now you've got no choice? Frightened now I won't be there for ya?
Mick Ya were 'ardly there anyway.
Kelly Only 'cos I can't stand ya.

Mick An' d' ya think I'm arsed?
Kelly I think you're a shit. I think ——
Mick Go on.
Kelly I think you're a worthless scab an' you've got no 'ope of gettin'
    anywhere unless ya stand on people's shoulders or walk all over them or
    get them pregnant ——
Mick Well you can't even manage that.
Kelly Not with you, thank Christ. At least me body's got sense.
Mick So you've got someone else lined up 'ave ya?
Kelly I've got me own life to lead first.
Mick What? On picket-lines?
Kelly Rather be a picket than a scab.
Mick Rather be a scally than a snob.
Kelly I 'ope they treat ya like shit.
Mick I'm used to it, livin' with you.
Kelly You'll be glad a the change then.
Mick Too fuckin' right I will.

*Josie and Bruce enter, holding hands. Josie has a metallic helium balloon
with a "love" message on it tied to her wrist*

*Bruce sits in the plastic chair and fixes his shoe. Josie stops beside him for
a moment and then enters the caravan*

Kelly God knows what you'll do without me to sponge off.
Mick D'ya think I need it? I only took it 'cos it was there.
Josie (*to Kelly*) What's goin' on?
Kelly Ask 'im.
Josie What's 'appened?
Mick Nothin'. We 'ad a bit of a row.
Kelly Bit of a row? You woulda smashed the place up given 'alf the chance.
Josie (*calling*) Bruce! (*To Mick and Kelly*) An' what about the neighbours?
    They've got little ones. I 'ope they're out.

Bruce enters the caravan

Ya should be bloody ashamed.

Josie begins to clear up the remainder of the plates and food

Kelly I am. I'm ashamed of 'im.
Bruce What's been goin' on?
Josie Domestic.

Kelly No it's not. It's 'im. It's 'cos a what 'e's done.

Bruce You 'aven't touched 'er, 'ave ya?

Mick It was just a row.

Kelly Just a row? Just you wait. 'Cos ya see 'im, 'e can't even get a job without bein' sly.

Josie These plates were me Auntie Ada's.

Kelly I couldn't give a shit while there's a scab sittin' 'ere.

Josie What?

Kelly 'E's bin took on at the docks, Bruce. 'E's a scab.

Silence

Bruce You been there today?

Mick I start Mondee.

Bruce Ya can't. Ya can't start. You can't go down to them gates an' walk through. Ya can't take someone else's life — 'cos that's what you'll be doin'.

Josie Did the dole push ya into it, son?

Bruce Doesn't matter if they did. 'E should 'ave the sense not to do it. Bein' a scab when ya own wife goes on the picket-lines —

Kelly I'm not 'is wife.

Josie Don't talk wet, Kelly.

Kelly D'ya think I'm gonna stay married to that? You should 'ave more sense, it could be Bruce's job 'e's takin'.

Josie At least 'e's tryin'.

Mick I just thought we could save up an' that.

Josie See. Ya moan when 'e doesn't work.

Kelly Well why didn't 'e find a decent job?

Mick There's nothin' goin' in my line of work.

Bruce Praps ya should carry on lookin'.

Mick There's no jobs nowhere.

Kelly 'E's only took this one to get at me.

Bruce Ya not gonna do it, are ya?

Mick I've never 'ad a job. I got the job, I'm gonna do it.

Bruce I'm on the line Monday.

Josie You'll 'ave to go a bit later so ya won't see 'im.

Bruce I won't see 'im anyway because as far as I'm concerned he doesn't exist.

Kelly 'E 'asn't existed for ages in my eyes.

Mick Don't I know it.

Kelly I've been workin' 'ard, it's you who plays around.

Josie Staffordshire Crown Pottery.

Mick You've been workin' 'ard, 'ave ya?

Bruce She's been fightin' a cause.

Mick An' won't let anyone forget it.

Bruce I didn't think you were the type to remember. But sorry, son, I never forget.

Bruce exits

Mick That strike's ruined what we 'ad.

Kelly That was already ruined. You were never interested.

Mick I must a been, I married ya.

Kelly An' that was it. That was all ya did.

Josie Kelly, keep ya voice down.

Kelly I will not. It was you who said marry 'im. Ya only concerned about bein' respectable.

Josie I am not. What about Kim? I didn't make 'er do anythin' she didn't want to.

Kelly Well in 'er case, p'raps ya should.

Josie She was only a kid but she knew her own mind.

Kelly Shit. I was supposed to pick 'er up.

Josie What?

Kelly She took the baby the doctor's.

Josie You've left 'er stranded with the baby?

Kelly She'll 'ave got the bus by now.

Josie You'd better go, just in case.

Kelly She'll be back in a minute.

Mick 'E was burnin' up an' all.

Kelly You go an' meet them if ya that concerned.

Josie Poor little bugger.

Kelly Don't make me feel worse than I already do.

Mick 'E's a baby for God's sake.

Kelly I notice 'ow ya capable a talkin' about that baby.

Mick What?

Kelly That baby a Kim's. Ya can talk about 'im. Why's that, eh? I know why. Why don't ya just say? Why don't ya tell us?

Mick What?

Kelly Say it. Go on, say it. It's obvious.

Mick No.

Kelly I know why. I know why ya talk about it!

Mick 'As she told you? She 'as, 'asn't she? I knew it.

Josie Told 'er what?

Mick I knew she would. I knew she'd ruin it. It 'appened before you. It just 'appened an' then she 'ad the kid. That was that. But she never let it go. It just 'appened an' that was that. But it was 'er — she just wouldn't let it go—

Josie Oh my God.

Kelly (*quietly*) I was only gonna say — Ya can talk about 'im but you've
never talked about ares. I knew there was someone — but Kim? It's been
Kim all along 'asn't it? Kim an' the baby. Ya wanted 'er but ya ended up
with me?

Josie I 'aven't even got a ciggie.

Mick It wasn't like that ——

Kelly That's your baby. You must think I'm stupid ——

Mick No. I've always wanted you. I wanted ya when I met ya ——

Kelly An' so must she. You must a been laughin' at me all the time.

Mick Kelly, no. I just never thought ——

Kelly Get out ——

Mick I never thought ——

Kelly Just get out, get out ——

Josie Go, Mick. Go an' meet 'er an' the baby.

Pause

   Mick exits

Kelly 'E ruins everythin'. Everythin' I 'ad. Ruins everythin'. Me whole life…

Josie Come on, love. Sit down.

Kelly 'E does.

Josie Not everythin'. 'E can't ruin everythin'.

Josie sits down and puts her arm round Kelly

Kelly 'E already 'as.

Josie No, 'e 'asn't. Not everythin'. (*Pause*) Me an' Bruce got engaged today.
Thought it was about time we made things a bit more permanent. (*Pause*)
No ring, like. The balloon 'ad to do. (*Pause*) What d' ya think?

Kelly All I can smell is fishcake.

Josie I thought you'd like 'avin' Bruce round permanent?

Kelly Yeh.

Josie So 'e 'asn't ruined it all. There's that to look forward to. One family,
one 'ouse, one caravan.

Silence. Kelly continues to cry

Act II, Scene 5 67

SCENE 5

Wives and Lovers

Music: "Wives and Lovers" by Jack Jones

The caravan. An early evening in late September 1996

It is raining softly. Kim sits on the side settee, she reads a magazine. Mick sits on the back settee watching the television. There is a "For Sale" sign displayed outside the caravan

Kim (*reading*) "Make your own trendy flower pots — just wash your empty food cans, peel off the label and fill them with your favourite plant. The (*she struggles*) alu-min-i-um will make a lovely contrast to the plant's colours and will brighten your home in no time." Sad bastards. Imagine 'avin' bean tins all over the flat.

Mick Yeh.

Kim Bet are Kelly'ld do that, given 'alf the chance. At least me mum's got sense. She'd put them straight in the bin.

Mick Or recycle them.

Kim Me mum?

Mick Kelly.

Kim I was gonna say, what would me mum wanna use a tin again for? But 'er. I could see 'er washin' them out an' puttin' more beans in, couldn't you?

Mick Not use them, recycle them.

Kim What d'ya mean?

Mick Throw them away an' then they get used again.

Kim So someone takes them out ya bin an' uses them again? That's fuckin' disgustin' that. Ya'd never know whose bin ya tin 'ad been in.

Mick Yeh. (*He laughs*)

Kim What?

Mick What?

Kim What are ya laughin' at?

Mick Nothin'. Just the tele.

Kim I 'ate it when ya do that.

Mick What?

Kim Laugh at somethin' that's just not funny.

Mick It was funny, you weren't watchin'.

Kim I 'eard it. It wasn't funny.

Mick I don't get much chance to watch the tele. Can't I watch it in peace?

Kim Thank God ya don't.

Mick That's nice. Ya'd rather me in work, all day every day, breakin' me back?

Kim Ya are anyway.

Mick An' that's why I like I comin' 'ere an' gettin' a bit a peace if I ever get the weekend off.

Kim I was only sayin'.

Mick Well don't say.

Pause

Kim Ya wouldn't break ya back though, would ya?

Mick What?

Kim In work. Like that fella.

Mick What fella?

Kim The one who broke 'is back.

Mick It was a accident. Accidents 'appen.

Pause

Kim Me mum said there was no accidents when the real dockers worked there.

Mick 'Ow would she know?

Kim Bruce said.

Mick 'Ow is it that whatever 'e says ya mum believes?

Kim 'Cos she's engaged to 'im.

Mick You're engaged to me but you don't believe nothin' I say.

Kim She's got a ring though.

Mick So will you when me boat comes in.

Kim Don't you rob one off a ship. I'm not wearin' a knock-off ring.

Mick When I've got the money.

Kim An' when will that be? When bettin' shops shut? (*Pause*) Didn't even know there was jewellery ships.

Pause

But ya will make sure ya won't 'urt yerself, won't ya?

Mick No-one's 'urt themselves.

Kim 'Ow come that fella's paralysed an' that other fella's got 'is leg in plaster? An' 'ow come your mate broke 'is arm?

Mick Both 'is arms.

Kim See. I knew it was true.

Mick What's she been sayin'?

Kim That ya should be careful 'cos there's loads of accidents cos youse
aren't real dockers.
Mick She would say that.
Kim Why?
Mick If I pack the docks in she can 'ave 'er 'appy family back again.
Kim An' are Kelly'd really like that?
Mick But, ya mam'd be gainin' two an' losin' one.
Kim Never thought a that. P'raps she was lyin'.

Pause

Take ya feet off there, Mick.
Mick You what?
Kim I'm responsible.
Mick What for?
Kim For keepin' it tidy. We've got to make it seem like we want someone
to buy this. You go treatin' it like it's ares an' me mum'll soon get wind that
we want it. Big stains on the couch are a dead giveaway.
Mick Me shoes are clean.
Kim That's not the point. I'm not losin' this caravan 'cos a your dirty feet.
Ya wouldn't do it if me mum was 'ere.
Mick I'm not doin' no 'arm.
Kim Take them down.
Mick No.
Kim Put ya feet on the floor.
Mick What for?
Kim 'Cos I said. Ya can't go treatin' like it's ares. Not yet. Anyway, you've
even started doin' it at 'ome, in case ya 'adn't noticed ——
Mick I 'adn't.
Kim — on the new three-piece.
Mick In me socks.
Kim They're still feet.

Josie enters. She carries two shopping bags filled with groceries

Mick Are you sayin' I should be on me best be'aviour in me own 'ome?

Josie enters the caravan

Josie 'Iya.

Mick takes his feet off the settee

Mick 'Iya.

Kim You do my 'ead in.

Josie Brought ya some stuff. Ya 'aven't 'ad ya tea 'ave ya? Went the big Co-op, spent a fortune. 'Ope Bruce doesn't notice the hole in me cheque book.

Kim An' where was the baby?

Josie unpacks the bags

Josie Bruce an' Kelly minded 'im. I got the bus. I'm fuckin' knackered. Runnin' round all fuckin' day. An' I brought ya washin' with us. It's in Bruce's. All ironed. I'll bring it after. I'll sneak it out. I 'ad to sneak out with this lot an' that was 'ard enough. I got ya Irish Cheddar instead of red Leicester. That'll make a change on ya butties.

Mick Ta.

Kim An' where is 'e now?

Josie 'E's in Bruce's van. 'E's well away.

Kim puts some shopping away

Kim You've left 'im with them all day?

Josie 'E's fast asleep. They've 'ad 'im on the beach lookin' for shells. The little fella's worn out. Bruce got 'im a bucket. 'E's got all 'is shells an' pebbles an' little dead crabs in it. 'E was made up they said. They were there for hours.

Kim 'N' what are ya leavin' 'im with them all day for? They'll 'ave 'im brainwashed.

Josie In case you 'adn't noticed, I've bin runnin' round after you all day. I 'ad to do your ironin' ——

Kim I would a done that ——

Josie Ya 'aven't got an iron.

Kim I would a done it if I 'ad one.

Josie I 'ad to do ya shoppin'. I can't do that with them around, they'd go ballistic.

Kim Well that's their problem ——

Josie It's my problem. I'm the one who's got to sneak about everywhere. D'ya want cheese an' onion, Mick?

Josie throws Mick a packet of crisps

Mick Ta.

Kim Well we can't go out, Mick's a scab.

Mick I'm a dock worker.

Kim A scab dock worker an' ya can't go out an' neither can I. That's what
I meant ——

Mick Only where people might know me or durin' the day when we might
be seen ——

Josie That gives ya plenty a scope —

Kim So it's not my fault that you've got to do me shoppin' even in Wales,
is it?

Josie No. It's 'is.

Kim I knew you'd start thinkin' like they do.

Josie Bruce is my fiancé. But that doesn't mean I'd turn me back on you. I
wouldn't do that. Not 'cos of 'im, not 'cos of any of it.

Kim Are you sayin' 'e's a scab?

Mick You've just said I'm a scab.

Kim That was different.

Josie I'm ya mother. I'll 'elp no matter what. I even got you ya favourite
noodles but to get them I 'ad to go to the shops. An' to go the shops I 'ad
to leave the baby with Bruce.

Kim I just don't want them fillin' his 'ead with lies an' loadsa shite.

Josie Be thankful they 'aven't been round an' filled Mick's 'ead with a
pickaxe. It was three for two on the biscuits. They'll do ya for when ya get
'ome.

Kim opens a packet of biscuits and takes one

Kim (*eating*) I don't want them sayin' that 'is dad's gonna get 'imself killed
or worse. Lyin' like they 'ave bin doin'.

Josie Are Kelly loves the bones of that baby.

Kim Wouldn't put it past them.

Josie But there 'ave been accidents, 'aven't there, Mick?

Mick Yeh.

Kim You said there 'adn't.

Mick But there 'ave. I can say it but a picket can't. If a picket says it or a paper
says it or the tele says it, it's a lie.

Josie Instead the papers an' the tele say nothin'.

Mick Better than lyin'. What ya don't know won't 'urt ya.

Josie Well Kelly wouldn't say nothin' to the baby.

Kim Just make sure ya bring 'im back after.

Josie I will. An' 'is bucket. Kelly said 'e's made up with it.

Kim She would. All them natural ingredients.

Mick Apart from the plastic.

Kim Ya know what I mean.

Josie At least ya should 'ave a quiet night with 'im, thanks to them. I'll see
ya later.

Kim D'ya want money for that?

Josie No.

Kim Ya sure?

Josie Don't be soft. Bruce might as well spend all 'is life savin's as 'alf a them.

Kim Ta.

Josie They must think I've bin losin' me touch. I told them I was in the bingo. I 'aven't got a thing to show for it. Ta-ra, Mick. Ta-ra, love.

Kim Ta-ra.

Josie (*as she exits*) An' don't forget, keep this place spotless 'cos the office told me there's an interested party. So ya never know — Ta-ra.

Josie exits

Kim I told ya you'd take ya feet down if me mum was 'ere.

Pause. Josie stands outside the caravan. Kim sits on the side settee and picks up her magazine

She doesn't know nothin', does she? Did ya 'ear 'er? "Interested party." Imagine when she finds out it's us. Ya won't be puttin' ya feet on the seats then, will ya?

Mick When it's ares I can do what I like.

Kim Ya better not ruin it 'cos we'll 'ave it lovely — like a palace. We'll get rid of all this an' 'ave it the way we want it. Do it all out, 'ave it all nice. We can rent it out then. That's what people want — nice caravans with nice insides.

It starts to rain harder

Mick As long as we make somethin' out of it.

Kim We will. She's more or less givin' it away.

Mick Only 'cos she's got to.

Kim An' I wouldn't want all are savin's goin' into their pockets. Imagine it, Mick. Soon we'll 'ave a permanent caravan to come to.

Mick I've worked 'ard enough for it.

Kim Ya know what? When we buy this, me dad'll be 'appy. 'E'll look down an' 'e'll be dead 'appy. 'E'll look down an' 'e'll know that I've always wanted this caravan. I'm gonna 'ave it like a palace.

Pause. Mick watches television. Kim resumes reading

(*Reading*) "Why not make use of your empty chocolate spread jars. Just clean them out when empty and start collecting them. They make ideal and inexpensive whisky tumblers." Why can't they just go the Fifty Pence shop an' buy some? Stupid gets.

Pause

D' ya know what? I can't imagine life without this place.
Mick What?
Kim The caravan.
Mick Why?
Kim 'Cos then we wouldn't 'ave nowhere to go.

Kim reads. Mick watches the television. Josie stares out front. Mick laughs

Black-out

FURNITURE AND PROPERTY LIST

ACT I

Scene 1

On stage: Two settees
Cupboard: *In it*: beach bag containing towel and **Kim**'s clothes
Radio-cassette player
Convertible bed. *On it*: child's duvet cover, sheets, pillow, cuddly
    Garfield toy
Table. *On it*: newspapers, crockery, food (packets of biscuits, bags of
    fruit bananas, apples, oranges etc.)
Crockery and cutlery in kitchen area
"For Sale" sign
Two gas canisters

Off stage: Two mint-choc chip ice-creams (one half-eaten) (**Mick**)
Bags of bingo prizes and cuddly toys (**Josie**)

Personal: **Josie**: packet of cigarettes, lighter

Scene 2

On stage: As Scene 1

Off stage: Make-up bag. *In it*: hand mirror (**Kelly**)
Hairbrush (**Kelly**)
Bumbag. *In it*: lipstick, keys, money (**Kelly**)

Scene 3

On stage: as before

Off stage: Case (**Mick**)
Larger case (**Kelly**)
Small bag. *In it*: keys, newspaper, tiny stretchy dress (**Kelly**)
Suitcase (**Josie**)
Holdall (**Kim**)
Cake box containing cake (**Kim**)
Four-pack of lager (**Kim**)

Scene 4

Strike: Cake, cake box, plates etc.
               Lager
               Kelly's bag, newspaper dress and keys

Off stage: Baby in carry chair (**Kim**)
               Asda bag containing soft Power Ranger toy, *Liverpool Echo* (**Kelly**)
               Cup of tea (**Josie**)
               Large holdall. *In it*: cans of beer (**Mick** and **Kim**)

Personal: **Josie**: cowboy hat
               Josie: packet of cigarettes, lighter

ACT II

Scene 1

Set: Two white tubs containing flowers
               Two garden gnomes pulling moonies
               Plastic table
               Two chairs
               Newspaper
               Betting slips
               Sealed bucket "Support the Dockers"

Strike: Holdall
               Cans of beer
               Asda bag
               Newspaper
               "For Sale" sign

Personal: **Kim**: betting slip

Scene 2

Set: Large cardboard box
               Piles of leaflets
               Pen, lists, paperwork etc.

Strike: Newspaper
               Bucket

Off stage: Make-up bag, with mirror (**Kim**)

Personal: **Josie**: packet of cigarettes, lighter

SCENE 3

Set:	The *Mirror* newspaper
	Josie's freezer-bag containing food parcels in foil, one large parcel
	contains cheese sandwiches
	Thermos flask
Strike:	Make-up bag
Off stage:	Inexpensive women's magazine (**Kim**)
Personal:	**Josie**: sunglasses

SCENE 4

Off stage:	Two parcels of chips and fishcakes (**Mick**)
Personal:	**Josie**: metallic helium balloon with "love" message

SCENE 5

Re-set:	Plates and crockery
Set:	**Kim**'s magazine
	Television
	"For Sale" sign
Strike:	Freezer-bag, food parcels
	Thermos flask
Off stage:	Two shopping bags with groceries, crisps, packets of biscuits (**Josie**)

LIGHTING PLOT

Property fittings required: main light in caravan. TV light effect
Interior (with exterior visible) the same throughout

ACT I, SCENE 1. Rainy October afternoon

To open: Overall general lighting

No cues

ACT I, SCENE 2. Morning

To open: Overall general morning lighting

No cues

ACT I, SCENE 3. Evening

To open: General evening lighting on caravan exterior

Cue 1   **Kelly** switches the light on   (Page 19)
            Snap on caravan interior lighting

Cue 2   **Kelly** switches the light off   (Page 21)
            Snap off caravan interior lighting

Cue 3   **Josie** switches the light on   (Page 22)
            Snap on caravan interior lighting

ACT I, SCENE 4. Bright evening

To open: Overall general bright evening effect

No cues

ACT II, SCENE 1. A dull afternoon

To open: General dull afternoon effect

No cues

ACT II, SCENE 2. Morning

To open: General overall lighting

No cues

ACT II, SCENE 3. Bright summer's day

To open: General bright lighting

No cues

ACT II, SCENE 4. Evening

To open: General evening effect

No cues

ACT II, SCENE 5. Early evening

To open: General early evening effect. Snap on TV flicker

Cue 4   **Kim**: "… nowhere to go." *When ready*   (Page 73)
                 Black-out

EFFECTS PLOT

ACT I

Cue 13	**Kim** turns on the radio	(Page 41)
	Radio race commentary as pp.41-43	
Cue 14	**Kelly** turns up the radio	(Page 42)
	Increase commentary volume	
Cue 15	**Kelly** turns down the radio	(Page 42)
	Decrease commentary volume	
Cue 16	**Kelly** turns off the radio	(Page 43)
	Cut radio effect as p.43	
Cue 17	**Kim** turns on the radio	(Page 43)
	Radio commentary as p.43	
Cue 18	**Kim**: "Rough bloody Quest!"	(Page 43)
	Cut radio effect	
Cue 19	To open SCENE 2	(Page 43)
	Music: "I Just Don't Know What To Do With Myself"	
	by Dusty Springfield. Fade when ready	
Cue 20	**Kelly**: "No slippin' the bingo."	(Page 45)
	Sound of hairdryer in Josie's room	
Cue 21	**Kelly**: "I've got that many lists."	(Page 46)
	Cut hairdryer effect	
Cue 22	**Josie**: "'E's out every chance 'e gets."	(Page 47)
	Sound of hairdryer	
Cue 23	**Josie**: "Someone at these conferences."	(Page 48)
	Cut hairdryer effect	
Cue 24	To open SCENE 3	(Page 49)
	Music: "Promises, Promises" by Dionne Warwick.	
	Fade when ready	
Cue 25	**Bruce**: "What is?"	(Page 54)
	Sound of toilet flushing	
Cue 26	To open SCENE 4	(Page 58)
	Music: "Sticks and Stones" by Donna Fargo.	
	Fade when ready	

Cue 27   To open Scene 5   (Page 67)
            Music: "Wives and Lovers" by Jack Jones
            Fade when ready

Cue 28   Music fades   (Page 67)
            Bring up rain effect and background television effect

Cue 29   **Kim**: "… with nice insides."   (Page 72)
            Rain increases

Cue 30   Black-out   (Page 73)
            Cut rain and TV effects